Fishing for Dr Richard

BOB KIMMERLING

To my dear wife Enid, son Jack and daughter Lydia.
To my wider family whose paths criss-cross mine,
and to my family of faith wherever you may be:

A fishing story by one still learning how to cast a net,
but with the constant help of the Master.

Bob Kimmerling

Proceeds from this book will be donated to:
www.vineyardcommunity.org
Reg. charity in England and Wales 1143951

*With thanks to Nicola, Mark, and Mary Rondel
for allowing me to be with Richard in his last days.*

Fishing for Dr Richard

I loved this book and very much enjoyed eavesdropping on the conversational journey of these two friends. It always left me wondering what was going to happen next in this gentle yet exciting narrative.

I also found myself embarking on my own journey of discovery with God, or rather rediscovery. Some of the anecdotes are remarkable (and hard to believe if I hadn't known the writer), but when I turn back to the Bible, actually, it's there already - the almost outrageous depths of God's love in indefatigable pursuit of mankind, portrayed in Bible story after Bible story. The God of the Bible is just the sort of God who could be expected to make Himself known like that, in coincidences and unexpected events loaded with meaning, not unlike the stories of this book.

Sometimes we need one another's stories to catch the truth. The delight of reading this book has caused me to look afresh at biblical teaching as if I'd never really registered the words before, nor really taken in how amazing the Christian story is. It has made me realise there is a whole depth and breadth of 'knowing God' yet to discover.

— Melanie Thomas
Retired botanist and member of the author's church.

"Come, follow Me," Jesus said,
"and I will make you fishers of men."

Contents

vii

Foreword

This was an unexpected adventure. I had thoughts of writing something but didn't imagine that it would take nearly six years. What transpired was a friendship that followed a chance encounter, and which was to become one of the great privileges of my life as Dr Richard and I found companionship in this adventure.

It was to become a pilgrimage, one of exploration and discovery, but with a destination that neither of us could have planned in advance, nor known the route by which we were to travel, though, in all of it, we ventured no more than a mile or two from our homes.

Fishing for Dr Richard was to become a book of the exploration of our lives, our faith, our growing love for one another, and foremost, an exploration of the love of God as two men approach the uncertainties of later life.

Richard's background was village church, choirboy and all the traditions of Christian faith, votive candles, and good living. Mine was a family without faith until I had a profound and unexpected encounter at the age of 22.

In this book, we travel those different paths together, and those who read ahead to journey with us are welcome to eavesdrop on our conversations. The reader may recognise some of their own thoughts, or they may, as I hope, head to further horizons where God's love beckons.

This book is written with enormous gratitude, and 'con un ultima fuerte abrazo', with a final big hug for Dr Richard.

— **Bob Kimmerling**

Chapter 1.

A Kentish Lad

The boys on the bridge were pulling out tiddlers. I could see them flashing in the morning sun while sitting on my mother's lap a little way down the bank. My mother wore a fifties cotton print blouse, with her farm headscarf wrapped and tied at the back of her head. The bridge was made of rough planks spanning steel girders across one of the many marsh dykes that criss-crossed towards the Great Stour River and the Kent coast. It was just a tractor pass between fields, where the ends and edges of loose planks lifted and clattered when tractors and trailers went over. Three boys sat dangling their rods and their legs, all reflected in the narrow dyke not far below their feet.

This is a random memory, a photo in the mind, with no continuity before or after. Rather more than sixty years forward, the image of that morning has not faded, though the sense of frustration at catching nothing belonged only to the child.

My mother had taken me fishing. Her farm cottage was deep in the Kent countryside, not far from Sandwich Bay and the sea, and where plenty of little dykes were home to little fish, and perhaps bigger ones, though at only five years old, I found no way to explore that.

Uncle Michael had made a cane rod with a cotton line, a cork float, and a hook. There must have been some family discussion because it was decided that a young lad might damage himself with a real hook, and so one of those old brass curtain hooks was attached at the end of the cotton line. The hook was round-ended and entirely blunt and it would have been difficult to snag a thorn bush let alone a fish, even more so a tiddler, and so seeing the slightly older boys pull out several fish, one after another, was frustrating. Adding to the complete improbability of my catching anything was the oversight of any bait. There was no bait on the hook.

When I was five or six, I graduated to bending pins for hooks, along with whittling sharp sticks for spears, making catapults and blow darts, and generally roaming the open fields. I had great freedom to explore and to adventure. Brother Tony was two years older and, when not at school, we threw stones at the tethered bull, crossed dykes in leaky barrels, and hitched rides on the back of the dung cart. As a farmhand, my father laboured nearly every day of the week and we two brothers roamed here and there as we pleased, not minding the dangers of farm machinery, or the silage pit, or collapsing hay bales in the barn.

There was also no fear of traffic since the country lane by the cottage had almost no cars passing by. From the age of three, I could walk with my brother about two miles along that lane to a school pick-up which completed the rest of the journey. Out of school, we disappeared for hours into surrounding orchards and fields and by the age of five, I had learned to make crude and generally ineffective weapons and attempted to shoot any creature that moved in open country or perched in the trees. I never hit anything that I intended to, but as soon as I could wander, the hunter in me was awakened, and the country freedom and solitude began to shape my character.

Two years was a big gap for brothers so young, and so, mostly, we went off alone. Tony once disappeared for the whole night until his white hair was seen bobbing through long grass the following day. There must have been some anxiety, but my mother's retelling never conveyed much drama. There was certainly no fear of stranger danger; it was a rare day to see anyone at all. I don't think anyone called the police for my missing brother. I don't think there were any police. There were certainly no phones.

When the Cheesemans visited one afternoon, I had just thrown half a broken spade handle at my brother. It was a children's beach bucket and spade, the kind with a red plastic paddle end and wooden 'T'-top handle that had met with an accident and had its shaft snapped in two. The previous day, I had won a small brightly coloured plastic ball at school sports day, a rare prize since nothing like that was available in the nearest shops, but Tony kicked it innocently into a strawberry patch as we were playing in the backyard. It was only a small patch of strawberries, but the ball disappeared and refused to be found. I was so furious that I picked up the nearest thing to throw at him. He was some way across the garden, so I was surprised that the broken spade handle hit him right on the head with the sharp broken point, a rare piece of accuracy that caused a deep gash. My misdemeanour resulted in a swift whack from Father, and I was sent upstairs to our bedroom just as the Cheesemans were arriving.

The whack was not the issue, I didn't mind it so much, but being sent upstairs and missing the entire Cheesemans' visit was real punishment. It's not that I knew who the Cheesemans were. I had no idea who the Cheesemans were. We had never seen them before or since. But the thing was, no one else had ever visited. Apart from older Cousin Dick, who once stayed a few days when I was still in my cot, and this visit of the Cheesemans, I don't remember anyone else visiting our home in those first six years of my life.

Sparrow Castle, as this rather grandly named thatched cottage was called, at first had no water or electricity, just a brick well out back with a rotting wooden lid intended to protect us from falling in. The cottage stood four square with whitewashed walls and small, black-framed windows. It didn't have a front door. As a farm cottage, the back door was the only one, and it opened towards a large yard - you couldn't really call it a garden - and this yard was enclosed by a dilapidated wire fence. When going outside, it was generally a good idea to exit quickly into the yard since the thatched roof was infested with sparrows and they seemed to have a habit of pooping on anyone who lingered too long at the threshold.

It was at this threshold that I have memories of my mother wringing chickens' necks, or occasionally chopping them off. Once in a while, the despatched and headless birds ran around the yard by neurological impulse before being gathered up from where they dropped. Mother then plunged them into a boiling pan to scald before she plucked and gutted, releasing that unpleasant and pungent smell of giblets and organs as I stood close by on a chair watching my mother as she worked quickly in the Butler sink. Sometimes, the chicken was roasted for a Sunday lunch, or perhaps a birthday treat.

No food was ever left to waste, and to my father's later regret, he once forced me to finish a calf's liver lunch. For well over an hour, I was not released from the table to play while I gagged as he force-fed me what I desperately wished to refuse.

The yard had a large willow tree, the well, the chickens in their coop, and also a detached wooden garage at the end of a short gravel drive leading through a five-bar wooden front gate opening from the single-track lane fronting the cottage. The shiplapped garage doors were peppered with scars where I practised my knife-throwing skills with half a pair of broken scissors, a defacing which parents did not seem to mind, and which occurred many years before the cottage became a converted and desirable country home with a new tiled roof.

My father parked his first car in the garage, his beloved split-screen Morris Minor, sky blue, and named Aggie. Most cars seemed to have been given female names back then. The top speed was around 60mph, with a blistering nought to fifty in twenty-nine seconds. Not that such speed was remotely possible in the narrow country lanes. I remember the car clearly, yet I have no memory of ever riding in it. I'm sure we must have, but I think outings were very few and far between and the seats retained their protective plastic covers.

There were orchards to the front but open fields behind the cottage, and visible on the near-flat horizon, several fields over, were two other farmhouses, well beyond the roaming of young boys. My mother's father's farm, Guston Elms, was one of them. It was the only arable farm amongst the Kent fruit trees and about a mile from our labourer's cottage sited just back from the Richborough Road, a lane bordered by tall hedges zigzagging between other farms half a mile apart. If we heard a rare car coming along the lane, we would run and stand on the bottom gate bar to watch it pass, maybe once or twice a day at most. In winter, sometimes with deep snowdrifts, there was nothing to even leave a passing tyre print.

From the age of three, Richborough Road was part of the long trek to school. I first walked two miles with my brother, past the Brussel's farm on a right-angle corner and on to the next junction at Cop Street, with its signpost to Westmarsh and Preston one way and Ash and Sandwich another. There we waited to be picked up to go the remaining mile or so to the Woottonley House school.

By that time in the morning, my parents had long been at work. Mum told of the pain of being trodden on by a heifer, and dad laboured with hundred-weight sacks of grain on his shoulders in the summer and picking Brussels sprouts with frost on them in the winter. He had once been gored in the head by a bull but got away without much damage, though his frame was ruined for later life by the heavy hessian grain sacks lowered by hoist onto his neck and back and staggered, sometimes two at a time, to store in the barn, sack upon sack. My father's role of marrying a farmer's daughter after the war and becoming a farmhand didn't sit well with him. It was extremely hard work and he hated it, especially the deep chill of hand-picking sprouts in the winter frost.

There had been an expectation that my mother would inherit the farm, but my grandfather had died before I was two and my mother's uncle Brough continued control through his share. He didn't die until just after my parents decided to leave for Cambridge in 1958, and just after my mother had sold out her inheritance for a fraction of what it was later worth.

Both my school headmistresses were animals, at the infant school in Ash and my later junior school headmistress in Cambridge, a Miss Cow and a Miss Hare respectively. At my infant school, the boy who sat with me to the left of my double flip-top wooden desk had complained that I had jabbed him in the arm with my pencil, which I had, but it was an accident. At least that is my memory of it, though probably not his. Miss Cow tied my hands behind my back with my school tie and hung me over the playground railings during a break; unthinkable nowadays, but no one batted an eyelid then. I was barely six years old.

When we had moved to Cambridge, Miss Hare at my junior school had invented another form of torture. I was particularly good at drawing and every picture seemed to deserve a reward. She would ask me into her study to praise every piece of good work. When I once drew a really good picture of a pike, coloured with its mottled markings and background of weeds, she invited me in for the usual 'well done' before saying, "And now I'm going to kiss you." She held my cheeks so that there was no escape and planted a kiss on my lips. I can remember feeling the spiky bristles on her upper lip and I saw other boys coming from her study wiping their mouths so I'm sure I wasn't the only one. I remember thinking it was better to be tied to the railings.

Mum had been a kennel girl when she met Dad and she was just 18 when they married. During the war, her father, Norman, Brigadier Norman Vause Sadler OBE, had been in charge of the anti-aircraft batteries at Dover and East Kent. He had shot down 90 planes in just five months in 1940, and in 1944, his artillery brought down many Doodlebugs, the V1 rockets. He saved a lot of lives, and London, from even greater destruction.

Norman was short, only 5'2", clean-shaven, square-jawed and a natural leader. The men under his command 'adored him', my mother had said, but she once told me that he had spoken to her saying that my father 'would be a good husband but amount to nothing.' I don't think my grandfather Norman knew how to give any fatherly love or encouragement to my mother. She had lost a child, christened Nigel, between my older brother and I, and her father Norman had said, 'Best not talk about it, old girl. Just get on with it.' That unresolved trauma came up in my mother's conversation most years, right up until her death aged 83.

My grandfather Norman was driving his parents in a car after the war when he had an accident and they both died. It must have been devastating and hard to recover from, but this was a generation of stiff upper lip and the avoidance of conversation about personal matters.

My father also came from a generation that lacked expression of intimacy. He was the youngest of five brothers, brought up on the shores of Lake Geneva in a grand house and estate called Lignon, until his father, Charles Albert, moved to Surbiton after the war. His brother, Oncle Albert, was a celebrated French aviator, and in 1911, was among the first to fly to a predesignated destination and back again, about 15 kilometres between Brons and Monceau, villages near Lyon. He was also the first to fly in the southern hemisphere, in 1909, at East London's Nahoon racecourse in South Africa, and perhaps the first to fly a female passenger, a reporter at that event.

Dad had been nurtured by his nanny Bundy and was ten years younger than his nearest sibling, Peter. There was then a gap of nine years to my Uncle Francois followed by the older brothers, Roger, and John. Mealtimes for the sons would require a stiff collar in order to be presented to their father whilst addressing him as 'sir.' In his last thirty years, Dad never had a single friend except for my mother. He was encouraged but never ventured out to anything social. He was always very welcoming when family visited, but he spent his days just pottering in his beloved garden or taking photographs, which he developed in a makeshift darkroom in the spare bedroom in their Cambridge home.

On a rare occasion, my father took my brother and me for a drink in the pub when we were teenagers. I was probably just old enough to have a legal drink, or at least look as though I might be eighteen. It was at the Fort St. George, a picturesque pub on the river Cam and within walking distance of our home. I don't remember anything about the conversation except this one thing, and I don't remember the context, but my father said, "I hate humanity in the mass." He said it in such a way that I knew he really meant it, and I remember being shocked and saddened and wondering why, though I didn't have the ability to question at the time. Perhaps it was the war.

I now think of perhaps the most well-known Bible verse, from John's gospel, the one that begins, 'for God so loved the world that he gave His only Son....' and I am saddened that my dad was so disillusioned and that his life was so barren. In some respects, his father-in-law's apparently heartless comment seemed to have been right.

I'm sure I must have had hugs from both parents, but I don't remember any demonstrable affection, except embracing my mother when she thought my father had died of a heart attack, though in fact, he went on for more than thirty years to potter in his garden. There had been one hug offered by my mother, which I rejected. She had tied a loose milk tooth to cotton and the other end of the thread to the pantry door handle before slamming it shut. It did the trick nicely, but I was not in the mood to accept her sympathy after the extraction and crossly pushed her offered hug away when she came to try to comfort me.

There had been scarcely any other children near the farm cottage. Judith was a slightly older girl at Potts Farm, along the Richborough Road in the opposite direction to the school, and there were a couple of even older girls at Guston Elms Farm, further still, but I had very few encounters. One such meeting was arranged with Judith. Someone, I suspect my mother, in cahoots with Judith's mother Sybil, had decided it would be a good idea for little boys to know what little girls looked like. A tin bath was filled in front of the drawing-room fireplace at Potts Farm and brother Tony and me, and also Judith, were made to sit in it while the lit fire took the chill off the room. Aged barely six, I didn't know what that was all about but there was no doubt we all felt great humiliation and asked to get out and be towelled dry very quickly.

Across several fields to the back of Sparrow Castle, the other farm that was visible on the horizon was the subject of occasional conversation. I had overheard my parents say that they were, 'the black sheep of the area', a bewildering expression for a youngster, but

I thought it was something to do with another word that was mentioned: 'alcoholism'.

I didn't meet my neighbour, Ian, that black sheep farmer's son who had lived across those fields, until I was a fresher at Nottingham University.

I was in the student buttery bar, we were all desperate to meet friends and fit in, and I was in conversation with the student sitting next to me. We were exploring backgrounds like, 'Where are you from?' 'Kent.'

'Oh, I'm from Kent too.' 'Whereabouts?' 'Near Ash.' 'Me too.' And so on, until we figured out that we had been back-door neighbours, the farm visible on the horizon. I took an instant dislike to Ian and he to me, and within a few minutes, I had poured my pint of beer over his head, not something I had done to anyone before or since.

Chapter 2.

Uncle Michael

I only fished that dyke near our farm cottage once. I didn't fish again at all until I was old enough to handle a proper rod and was on a school summer holiday visit from Cambridge to see my mother's brother and his wife Frances. Uncle Michael had borrowed some sea fishing gear from the fishermen who winched their boats on greased sleepers up and down the steep pebble beach at Deal. Michael had entered me for an angling competition on the pier, within sight of Eastwell House on the seafront, which contained my grandmother's top-floor flat and which he and my aunt Frances occupied after my grandmother had died.

Uncle had first caught sight of Frances after the war. She had survived horrific experiments in Belsen, but even with one lung, Frances was a beautiful woman and, at his first sight of her, Michael had declared to his mother: "That's the girl I'm going to marry." And so he did.

On the day they sent me off to the fishing competition, they watched the pier through binoculars from their window overlooking the seafront and they could see that at one point, towards the end of the competition, a crowd had gathered, seemingly around me. Naturally, they thought that I must have caught something special. In fact, it was the man next to me who had struck lucky.

Nearly all of those who were fishing on my side of the pier, myself included, had, one after the other, caught the bottom, or at least we had thought so. Some had managed to free their hooks and others had lost them. After freeing my hook, the man next to me snagged something nearly immovable, just like the rest of us had. He managed, however, to lift the dead weight and as something broke the surface, we could see that it was an enormous lobster. It must have been following the lines of bait along the seabed, from one hook to the next. I think the lobster was around 11lbs, and three feet across stretched claw to claw.

Watching through his binoculars, my uncle Michael had been excited for me, but I came home crying because every competitor had been promised a prize and somehow my name had been missed out at prize giving. He marched me back and with great indignation demanded something for me. They found a yellow plastic water pistol, a great treasure for a young boy in those days.

Michael and Frances were childless. My uncle was a surrogate father to me while my own father worked long hours on the farm, and also in later years when we visited from Cambridge, or I came down to Kent by myself to stay in the school holidays. Michael was an artist who taught me to draw and paint and since he was unable to work through long-standing illness, mostly tuberculosis, we spent time painting together. We were close in the kind of formal and mannered way that was appropriate for the time. Words to express our affection would not have been voiced, but I know we felt close to each other. He saw me as a son, and he was like a father to me.

Despite his illness, my uncle was a very upright and dignified man. At the dinner table I was made to have a ruler down my shirt back to make me sit up, hold my knife and fork correctly, and definitely never talk with a mouth full of food. Table manners and politeness were paramount. Michael was handsome, with his waxed moustache and full head of hair, always Brylcreemed and coiffed with a neat parting. When he wasn't in his painting smock and smelling of gum Arabic and turpentine, he always wore a shirt, a cravat, and corduroy trousers, and so did I on days out with him, also with parted, brushed and Brylcreemed hair.

We would have an occasional adventure together, and when I was old enough to visit art galleries in London, we dropped into the Park Lane Hotel for tea, a huge extravagance since he had little income. Before taking a seat, we visited the toilet. There were no urinals, only enclosed cubicles, which uncle always went into to empty his colostomy bag. We came out of the gents together and he realised that he had left a magazine inside, but looking up, we also realised that we had mistakenly used the ladies.

There was no one around, but Michael was too proper to knowingly go back into a ladies' toilet, and so he put his shoulder to block the outer entry door to the lobby while he sent me to run in and get the magazine. By the time I had found it and come out again, the door uncle was shoulder-blocking was being barged and buffeted from the other side. As soon as uncle saw me exit the ladies, he stood aside. A fine old gentleman, giving one final shove from the other side, came flying through and landed face down. Uncle retained all his composure and simply said, "Sorry, old boy, just one of those things." We didn't stop giggling for the rest of the day. We had such fun on our days out together, and I adored him.

It was a great shock when, aged seventeen, while I was at home in Cambridge watching weekend sport on our front room tv, my mother suddenly declared that she felt unwell. She said, "Something dreadful has happened!" and then she went straight upstairs to bed before teatime. Sometime later that evening, there was a phone call. Michael had blown his brains out with a shotgun in the garden shed of Pippin Cottage, their later home in the Kent countryside.

No one spoke to me about this great shock and my bewildered grief. No one explained to me that he had been dying and wanted to spare my aunt the indignity of his rotting insides and the smell that was coming from him. Nothing had been said. I stopped sleeping at night and began to feel sick whenever I went to school. I spent nights awake on my bed drenched in sweat, anxious and exhausted by what was happening to me.

There were then days at home excused from school. I would bang my head on the walls to try to relieve the mental torment that was building. I was having a nervous breakdown at the age of 17 and while my parents talked with each other, and with my headmaster, and with the doctor, and the doctor prescribed some placebos, no one ever talked to me.

It didn't last too long, thankfully. I decided to go fishing and fell asleep on my bike and fell off on the side of the road leading to Milton, and to Baits Bite lock where I would take myself off to fish at weekends. I didn't make it to the river that day, but I slept by the side of the quiet road where I had fallen, and, from then on, began to recover. Through all of this, and for some years after, no one ever talked about important things, and certainly, no one ever said anything about God. He didn't get a mention, let alone become a topic of conversation and it was to be another 5 years before God unexpectedly interrupted the course of my life, and another 42 before the adventure of this book began.

Chapter 3.

When Do We Begin?

Dr Richard came into the community centre one morning. It is in the basement below the Vineyard Life Church on a road called the Vineyard in Richmond. It was once frequented briefly by former Prime Minister Tony Blair, who ran live music discos there in his gap year before going to Oxford. He had no doubt heard of Richmond's mid-sixties music scene with the likes of the Rolling Stones and the Yardbirds at the Crawdaddy Club and Eel Pie Island, though by 1972, he was a little late to catch that same boat. Now, the centre is for those in crisis, or homeless or in food poverty. There is an afternoon coffee bar creating a community for the lonely and marginalised and many hundreds of local people from all walks of life drop in for various reasons.

Dr Richard was one of them. He was a big man. A phrase from Gerard Manley Hopkins' poem comes to mind, about the farrier Felix Randal: 'big-boned and hardy-handsome.' Except that Dr Richard did not have the rough hands of a smith; quite the opposite. His English was emphatically pronounced and slightly plummy, his manner very courteous, even at times excessively so to the point of diffidence if he thought directness was too impolite. Most of our encounters began with an unnecessary apology such as 'sorry to trouble you, Bob, - you're probably too busy - I don't want to intrude….'

Though he did have a big frame like farrier Felix, at six foot five (an inch less than his brother), the years had not yet shrunk him, and even his size fifteen shoes were getting too small for swelling feet. "Oh, it's ridiculous," he told me when I first noticed them as we sat together for a coffee, and he was wearing sandals on a cold day. "It's a bloody nuisance. I have to wear whatever I can get in that size; a great affliction."

Richard carried himself well and didn't yet have much of the stoop and shuffle of an old man approaching 84, and twenty years older than me when we first got properly acquainted at the centre. He still had a reasonable head of hair, slightly thinning but with plenty of colour left. We had been acquainted before, but I didn't know him at all well and he was carrying a plastic bag when he came into the café that first time.

"Bob, I know you're probably too busy to think about this, but I wondered if someone would like some fresh trout. They have only just come out of the water. I caught them this morning." He opened the bag to show me two beautiful rainbow trout, about a couple of pounds each, still iridescent and obviously just caught, as he had said.

That brief visit was repeated the following week, and then again, several times towards early summer, each time with one or two lovely trout that we could give to those who liked fresh fish and had a kitchen to cook them. At some point, I may have passed a comment that I was also a fisherman, but there was little time to chat, until one day, Richard found the opportunity to say, "Look, Bob, I know a chap like you is probably too busy, but if you fancy a trip with me, we could go together. I have another rod and reel and can sort all the stuff out for you." Later that day, Dr Richard dropped in some information about Ashmere Lakes in Shepperton. It lay on my desk for a few weeks until finally, we made a firm date to go one morning, and then to have lunch after fishing.

It was a beautiful day; we both caught two, and Richard showed me the rod room where rods in racks lined the walls, an old-fashioned upright scale sat in the middle of a large weighing table, and where we were required to record in the record book the fish weight and the fly which was used to catch them. I reckoned my largest that day was the bigger and he reckoned on his. In the end, the scales showed that I had it by a quarter of an ounce. One pound 13 ¾ ounces, on a blue flash black damsel. It was a great morning's fishing; we bought some quail eggs displayed for sale by putting a little money in an honesty box in an adjacent room and our friendship was growing. It was something quite rare for me considering our age difference and that my busy day to day life was mostly involved with people younger than myself.

We chatted over a simple lunch at the nearby Holiday Inn. We spoke about fishing and life, and his work as a doctor before retiring, and I must have told him something about my journey of faith. I think my conversation on a couple of occasions must have included something like, 'God spoke to me', or 'God said.'

Richard interrupted at one of these mentions, looked at me pretty intently and leaned forward. He said, "What do you mean? What do you mean, God spoke? Surely God doesn't speak, does He? Not anymore."

It was either that night or perhaps the following, that I lay awake. It seemed like all night, but it was probably only a couple of hours. As I lay awake, I suddenly thought of Richard and his comment, 'Surely God doesn't speak, does He?' For months, I had been thinking about taking time out to write. For several years, a few folks whom I respected have occasionally mentioned that perhaps I should try writing. Recent changes in my work made it possible to pencil in a month from mid-November and give it a try. I knew I had stuff that I wanted to write about and plenty of life stories, but I didn't have a way of putting it together.

That night, I had the thought that maybe I could tell my stories to Dr Richard. Maybe my book could be formed by our conversation, whereby I could explain to him that, yes, God certainly does speak, that He longs to walk and talk with us and enjoy our company. In a moment, I seemed to be quickened by the thought that it might work. Was it God's prompting? it seemed both clear and yet very uncertain. And then, what on earth would Dr Richard think of embarking on such a proposal?

The more I thought about it the more excited I got, but of course, it would need Dr Richard's cooperation, and somehow the understanding of what we might be getting into, even though he couldn't understand it, or at least he hadn't yet come to understand that God also wanted to draw close to him in friendship and communion.

Our second fishing trip was arranged for another morning. It was mid-June and a bright day when fishing isn't so good, but again we both caught, though this time just the one each, and I don't think we bothered to compete on the scales. I was nervous about lunch. I had planned to broach the subject of this book and to ask him if he would be interested in taking part. I had no idea what he might say or whether he would understand at all what I might have in mind. I had built up the kind of nerves you get when you ask a girl out on a date and I didn't really know what to say or how to say it but when the conversation slowed, I started.

"Richard, I'm thinking of writing a book and I'd like you to help me with it." He didn't seem at all surprised, but then, he didn't really get what I was saying. "Yes, of course," he said. "I've done quite a bit of proofreading and I will be happy to help. What's it about?"

"Well, it's about me," I paused, "and it's about you." He looked at me blankly. "I'd like us to go on a sort of pilgrimage, but not one where we actually travel. More like one where we travel through each other's lives and explore them together. A conversation between two old men, if you like. But I'd like you to know why I think God really does speak and why He wants to be close and intimate with all of us. And if the book is of any interest to others, it will be a bit like when someone is sitting at a coffee bar or a restaurant, and they're able to eavesdrop on the conversation next to them.

"I think the book might be something like that, Richard. And I don't want it to be planned or contrived. Let's not set an agenda so that we cover this topic today, and that one next week. I don't think God works in our lives with neat bullet points in a predictable sequence. I think He just enjoys relationships. Which one of us plans ahead our conversations with friends? Let's just meet and talk, and maybe walk together and enjoy each other's company, and do a little fishing. I think that's the way God would like it."

I took a deep breath and sat back. Richard stopped eating and slowly wiped his mouth with his serviette. He took several moments to compose his thoughts as he looked me in the eye while he was sat back in his chair. Then, he leaned forward very earnestly.

"Yes", he said. "I get it. When do we begin?"

Chapter 4.

Gods and Grails

We had our first coffee in the back garden of the Vineyard Community Centre, just off Richmond Hill. It's a quiet backwater when the morning drop-in is not open, and the business of the café lunch has also died down. Our common ground had been fishing and I asked Richard how he started.

"We were a Jersey family, Normandy originally, but grandfather's generation were the last to live there. My father came over when he was about 14 and fished before I was born. In Jersey, everyone fished.

"We lived in a house that, within two fields, went down to a very pretty little stream. Father took me down and I sat with him when I was four or five. We had two or three nice rods, proper tackle, and we fished with bread pellets for anything. In those days, every little tiddler was there, minnows, gudgeon, roach, even little stickleback.

"When Father thought we were getting on OK, he started us off on pike with a 7ft two-piece, a lovely little rod and reel, and we fished with live bait, or a little silver spoon polished one side with a triple hook with a red fluff dressing on it. That was behind the house a little way and we caught a lot of pike.

"My mother's father was a publican at Sawbridgeworth. Just behind the pub was a river alive with fish and we fished there a lot when we went to visit. In addition, my father's father retired (I would have been about eight) and they went down to Penzance and opened a big boarding house. Up until the war, we went down there each summer and fished. We either fished off the dockside in Penzance harbour or we fished at night off Newlin Pier where they had an overhanging light, and you couldn't help but catch pollock. In those days, Mousehole was still a tiny fishing village and just beyond the harbour there was a shelf of rock and going down the shelves, you could also fish for pollock and bass.

"Penzance had an inner and outer harbour and when the tide was out the inner harbour was totally exposed. Mud. We used to go down there with bare feet to fill a bucket of ragworms. You could catch anything with a ragworm, and we caught a lot of stuff off the dock. Up until maybe ten years ago, I had a photograph of my brother and me standing and holding up between us, at arm's length, a Conger eel that must have been about 5 feet long and my grandfather was shouting, 'Be careful, be careful! It'll break your arm!'

"That sort of thing went on until the war when there was no fishing, and then at the end of schooling, I went up to read medicine. I did three years at Kings College in the Strand and then went across to St. Georges for three years. Then I did my National Service in the army as a junior grade pathologist. I was posted to Cyprus for a year where I did a lot of scuba fishing and then to Gibraltar where I did the same. I didn't really start fishing again with rod and line until about 1969 when I was about 38 years old. We were near something called Frensham Pond. The children were little then, and they weren't that interested, but my career took over and from 1982, I did various medical research jobs in Europe - in Brussels, Munich, then Basel - and I didn't fish at all.

"In '92, I switched jobs and became an extremely successful consultant and an expert in something that not many people were at that time, and I decided that fishing in still waters was OK. However, I was beginning to get magazines through the post, and I decided that before I died, my Holy Grail was to catch an Atlantic salmon. I felt that the Atlantic salmon is a very extraordinary fish, I still do, and I was set on getting one.

"I went to Norway and for a week, I fished the Gaula, one of the big rivers that carry the Atlantic salmon. I stayed in a lodge owned by a man who had been centre half for Liverpool. But it didn't work very well for me and I caught nothing. Then I read that the Miramichi in New Brunswick had salmon. I had friends in Toronto and went to visit and since I was that far over, I phoned the Miramichi and the chap who answered said it was probably a good time because the fish were all at the mouth of the river waiting for the rain so they could come up. They can smell it and sense when the rains are coming so that they can go up and spawn. So, off I went and because I was then earning very well, I paid a lot of money and fished for a week.

"During that week, there wasn't a drop of rain and all the salmon stayed at the mouth and none of them were coming up at all. I fished with three big shots from a law practice in Carolina, but none of us caught a thing. So, the next time I was in Toronto, I had a mailshot from a lodge in a mini-mountain range called the Chic-Choc Mountains. From that range run a whole network of streams into the St. Lawrence Seaway and they are all characterised by gin-clear water, coming down through deeply forested rocky gorges. There's the St-Jean River in the Gaspe peninsula of Quebec and two or three others. Beautiful! There, I caught two nice salmon and I thought, that's that, I'd probably done it.

"Not long after, I knew a fellow who ran a sort of network and he would phone up and say, 'I've got two rods cancelled on so-and-so river, are you interested? He phoned me and said he had just had a call from Orri Vickfusson. Now, Orri is the god of salmon preservation, the president of the North Atlantic Salmon Federation and all sorts; lovely man, Icelandic. There was a message from one particular patron who, every year, books the prime week on the big Laxa, which is a river in Iceland that goes up north, drains off the glaciers and is full of salmon. He said, "Are you interested?" I said, "Well, dear Lord, do I take out a mortgage?" He said, "It's quite expensive but if you want to go away afterwards and never catch another salmon, that's the place to go."

"So, there I was, booked into *the* prime week in Icelandic Atlantic salmon fishing. I want to pick up this thing with you, Bob. I am a lucky man. Good things happen to me. So, I went up there and met Orri, someone I had known about for years, a god! I went up to the lodge, which was very luxurious, and he came out and greeted me and said, "Come and have a coffee," and we sat down and chatted for about an hour. I said, "I've fished for salmon before but believe me, I'm a rookie. I can't use a 15 ft rod and I'm not good at Spey casting. You know, if you're fishing on the Spey in Scotland, you'll be on the bank, or up to here in the water but the salmon are about 75 or 100 yards over there. So, you have this 15 ft rod, and you work up a long cast by performing a series of looping manoeuvres that generate the speed of the line. It's quite a complicated manoeuvre but it means that once your line is out there 75 yards, you can bring the line off the water and back on the water very promptly. It's really the only way you can deal with fish at a distance.

"I said that what I had with me was a nice 9 ft rod and to the extent that I catch a salmon at all, I will have to do it with a single-handed rod. He said, 'That's all right, I know just the guide for you,' and later that day, in walked Gutti, a 60-year-old plumber. All these Icelandic workmen have periods of the year when they guide and gillie for salmon. So, there was Gutti, and, for the six days that I fished, I've got the record at home, and I mustn't exaggerate, I hooked and lost seven or eight which I felt terrible about. Gutti said, 'Listen, listen to me, it happens.' But I hooked and landed, and put back again, eight beautiful salmon across a six-day period.

"Now, if you talk to people who take a week fishing in Scotland, one, you have to cope with a gillie who hates you, two, the chances are you won't catch anything for a whole week, and three, you'll have spent about twice what I spent in Iceland. So, I thought, right, that's that, that's probably it.

"Meantime, I had a friend who said he was going to try and buy a bungalow in Naples in Florida, was I interested? By then, I was halfway to retirement, and I said yes. We got this lovely brand-new bungalow about five miles from the sea. I used to go over there and fish for two or three weeks and fish all around the Ten Thousand Islands. As the Everglades drain south from Lake Okeechobee, it filters out through a myriad of channels into the Gulf of Mexico and the Ten Thousand Islands are mangrove bits that have dropped off and hook up to oyster beds and then start another mangrove island.

You go in and out of these little islands. It is total peace. I was hooked. I did a lot of fishing there for snook, redfish and groupers. I had a tarpon but lost it. All on fly. I had decided at an early stage in my fishing that *the* thing to do was saltwater fly fishing. That, I thought, is *it*.

"I tried and tried for tarpon and couldn't get one, but I had decided that tarpon was the next Holy Grail for me. So, I looked up the guides and the place to fish down the Florida Keys is called Islamorada. I found a guide there and I booked him for a week. The wind is always blowing there but it was blowing strongly that week and I couldn't get a fly out on the water. So, we used a spinner with a mullet fillet, but nothing happened. On my last day, we were due to dock at 5 pm, and at 3.30, I got into a huge tarpon. He kept me at it for about 35 minutes and eventually we brought it up alongside the boat. It was about 110 pounds, and about as big as I am, so I couldn't boat it. I couldn't hold it up for a photo in the water, so I said 'hello' to it, unhooked it, and let it go. So, that was that.

"I suppose I'm telling you something about myself, Bob, in that, yeah, that was nice, but it sort of left me nagging a bit and I thought, I haven't really done it. Then I was in Farlow's sports shop in Pall Mall where I got to know a lot of people and they got to know me and I told them about my tarpon and they said, 'Jolly good, jolly good,' but they said, 'You haven't fished for bonefish, have you? Well, you'd better not get too cocky until you've fished for bonefish.' So, Sean Clark, one of the blokes there said, 'Look, I'm putting a party together to go to Cuba next April, prime bonefish time. Would you like to come?'

"I had money then and I could afford it. Bonefish fishing is quite different to anything I've done, and Sean recommended reading Chico, an American who had produced this book about fishing for bonefish and how incredibly difficult it was. I read it and became immensely dispirited, but Sean persuaded me to buy in. So, I went with this Farlow's party to Cuba.

"Now, on these trips, everything is done in pairs. You book a room to share, and a guide. But I won't share a room; that's just me, I don't like to, so I paid the supplement and that meant I also had a guide and skiff to myself. My guide was Pedro who was brilliant. Out we went on the first day. You leave the dockside on the west side of Cuba, and you've got about a hundred miles of ocean. So, five skiffs go out, two men in a boat plus guide, me just one, and within ten minutes, you can't see any of them. I said to Pedro, 'Some of the guides get terribly upset if you don't catch because it reflects on them, but I fear you've drawn the short straw in me.' 'Oh,' he said, 'we'll see what we can do.'

"Fishing Cuba is a bit like fishing the Ten Thousand Islands in that it wouldn't matter if you didn't catch fish; it's entrancing. It's communion with the Great Spirit if you like. I'm not being blasphemous; you know what I'm saying, quite beautiful. And the flats have a mixture of stones and shingle, and it scintillates in the shallow water. It's like a kaleidoscope. I tried to photograph it, but you can't.

"So, out we went, and Pedro said, 'Right, I can see some bonefish over there. You get up on the front.' Pedro gets up on the platform at the back and sticks his pole in the mud and ties it. And then he says, 'There's bonefish at 10 o'clock, 45 yards!' I couldn't see a thing, but the guides are experts at seeing bonefish sitting just below the surface. Well, I didn't do too well for the first 15 minutes, but I got into the swing of it and within an hour I had caught the biggest bonefish of any of the party that week. Eight pounds; a beautiful fish. And I went on through the week to catch 40 bonefish. Now, you're not in the business of numbers, but if you're doing something for the first time and you've been told how difficult it is, it does sort of make you feel good to catch well. So, that was that.

"By then, I was beginning to feel the economic pinch and I thought that's probably the last trip I'll do. But then I met another chap in Toronto, a friend of a friend, one of these chaps who arranges fishing trips. He used to phone me up and I would say, 'No, I can't afford it!', but I told him about tarpon and my Holy Grail, and he called me with a trip he was arranging to Mexico. There's a town called Campeche on the Gulf, on the west side of the Yucatan Peninsula. When you go out from there, you are in a tarpon nursery. The fish start there and grow up to about 40 pounds and then they migrate into the big Atlantic streams. 'It's fun!' he said.

"So, I went to Campeche and the guide had just started a new fishing school. The guides were all fishermen who used to fish for prawns, but the prawn beds had all dried up, so they had to convert to something else. They knew the waters. He did the same as Pedro in Cuba.

"Tarpon are also difficult. Most tarpon you lose. In their mouths, they have bony plates like sandpaper, and they are very difficult to hook. Most of the time, they spit the hook out and they are quite difficult. You get out your line and then bang! But off they get. So, I hooked a lot of tarpon and I boated about eight or nine in the week.

"While I was there, I got bitten a lot, and when I came home, I was quite unwell a couple of weeks later. I went to see the G.P. who took some blood and got some fairly sniffy results back, as a result of which I was referred to the London School of Hygiene and Tropical Medicine. What I had got was one of the Rickettsia bacterium diseases, Rocky Mountain Spotted Fever; quite serious. I attended the School of Medicine for about 15 months until they got it sorted.

"And that was that. That was the end of my great fishing, my saltwater fly fishing, the love of my life. It ended about three years ago, and I do miss it."

Chapter 5.

Heidi Miracle

Richard's great passion for fishing had led him from one reminiscence to another. He was very animated about what was clearly a great joy. After each 'that was that', I expected him to conclude, but he did eventually run out of steam at the point of his tropical disease.

"Your coffee's getting cold, Richard. What about another one?" Richard glanced at his cup and took a sip. "No, it's still OK. But now, Bob, doing a replay of all this, my impression is that I've been rather self-indulgent in the way I've talked to you. The stories of a fisherman!"

"We have a lot in common, Richard. I've been near some of those places you talked about, though not Cuba or Iceland, and never fishing, but I owe my life to an Icelandic girl. Like your Orri Vickfusson, but in a different way, she was also God to me. Her name was Heidi, Heidi Miracle. I expect her surname was an assumed one, but I didn't think about that at the time."

I proceeded to tell Richard about Heidi, and how I was studying to be an architect in my last month at Nottingham University. Three years after I had poured my beer over the head of my childhood neighbour, I overheard a tutor speaking to another student saying, 'If I was a young architect now, I would try and get a year-out work experience with Norman Foster.' I had no idea who Norman Foster was, but I heard the tutor say this. After my first bachelor's degree I had to get some work experience, and so I thought, 'Right, that's what I'll do.'

I didn't realise that Norman Foster was fast becoming a famous architect, or that hundreds of other students might be trying for the same work experience with him, but my last piece of work was technologically innovative, and I decided to send it off to Foster Associates, as they were then called, and ask about whether it could actually work. To my surprise, I was invited to go to London and talk about it and I found myself round a table with Norman Foster and some engineers from Ove Arup. The outcome of that visit was that I ended up getting a job there for my student year out.

The practice in Charlotte Street, London W1, was still quite small. The ground floor facade of their office was one of the first in the UK made of curtain wall mirror glass, but a couple of years before, the IRA had bombed the nearby Post Office Tower and a large chunk of concrete had bounced on the pavement and gone through the office front to back. That aside, it was a pretty cool place to work for a young aspiring architect. I was placed under the wing of a Norwegian associate, Tom Nyhus. He was a macho man, good looking in a rugged sort of way and I suppose I felt a little in awe of him. His name was the equivalent to Casanova, as he often liked to remind me, and he had a beautiful wife who was 'all woman,' as he also often liked to remind me. It wasn't particularly helpful for a single young man of 21 but I was somewhat spellbound by my good fortune at landing on my feet in London.

There was a lot of office politics going on and Tom, who had brought the Norwegian Fred Olsen in as a client, was trying to make a name for himself. He took charge of me and tried to keep our work from Norman Foster's prying eyes. It turned out that Fred Olsen had commissioned a lot of work in Norway, and I think Tom must have been seeing his future back there. Two young Norwegian architects were also recruited to join us in London and about nine months into my year, we were all due to go out to Oslo to establish a new Foster office there, based at the old coal dock. We were going to design a large project aimed at relocating Fred Olsen's staff from their oak-panelled boardrooms in Oslo to an innovative and hi-tech eco-development at a forested site on the Oslo Fjord. It was something well ahead of its time for 1974 and I couldn't believe my luck at being part of it.

Just a few days before leaving for Norway, Norman and Tom spoke to me outside the office saying that they had changed their minds and that I would stay in London for my few remaining months. I was stunned and desperately disappointed. On the spot, I said, 'Well, in that case, I resign. But I'm going to go to Oslo anyway.' Now, this was not a calculated trump card. As a year-out student, I had no cards to play at all. I was just a spotty young man with three months to go in work experience, and I certainly had no means of carrying out such a rash decision. I was still very much discovering who I was and had little emotional security or confidence. I was, therefore, shocked at where my words had come from. And Tom and Norman were equally shocked.

We all stood there in silence and looking pretty shocked for quite a long time until Norman said, "Well, in that case, you'd better go for us."

It was in Oslo that I met Heidi. I had been given use of an apartment just to the west side of Oslo and my daily routine was to catch a bus and then walk across the open square at Fridtjof Nansens Plass towards the Akershus dock area, and then on to the old coal dock where we had converted a small office big enough for about four desks and drawing boards.

The first time Heidi approached me in the street as I made my daily journey to work, she spoke in Norwegian to me, and I shrugged my shoulders and walked on. The chances of her approaching me again the next day were very small, but she did so, this time on my return leg from the office, though I later realised that I was just another passer-by to her. It was not as though I had been recognised from the day before. This time, however, Heidi spoke to me in English.

I have no idea what she said but my eyes were transfixed by her lovely face, smiling and friendly, and for a young man, alone in a foreign country, and with nothing much to recommend him to a girl's attention, this was something quite unusual for me. It wasn't until sometime later that I even noticed she was very pregnant beneath her heavy dark duffle coat, of the kind with a hood and fastened by wooden toggles on cords.

I know now that it was God who had cast a line out for me on that day, and Heidi was the bait. She soon introduced me to some of her friends, something quite welcome in the midst of knowing hardly anyone in Oslo, with its long summer evenings lasting to midnight.

There was Asaph, a Norwegian, and Stephen, who was English, and several young people from various countries. When we met, they talked to me about God and about Jesus. I had never before heard anything like what they were saying. It seemed that they were part of something called Gud's Barn, Norwegian for 'Children of God', and their days were spent talking to people on the streets while they lived the summer in tents in nearby woods. Within a week, I was getting to know them and offered my flat for their baths and showers since they had nothing like that for themselves, though I had no idea at the time that these youngsters were soon to be led astray by their American cult leader known as Moses David. The movement had formed out of the Californian counterculture starting in the late sixties, including the Jesus Revolution amongst hippies, but they eventually embraced free sex and 'flirty fishing' for young folk like me, though I saw none of that in Norway.

As I began to wander around with them on weekends and after work, I started to realise that they had no money. They had nothing, in fact, but they seemed to pray about everything. If they needed to meet up with each other, they would just stop and pray and then one of them might say, 'We need to go here', or 'we need to go there', and sure enough, the group would meet up. If they needed to travel, they had no money for tickets, but on more than one occasion, there would be eight or ten of us on a train and if the inspector came on, they would quickly just pray together. 'Lord, blind his eyes to us!' The inspector would come down the train punching every ticket ahead of us and then miss every one of us out before checking the tickets of the passengers that followed on. I'm not recommending it, I'm just saying that's what happened, more than once, and I had no idea what to make of what my eyes were seeing.

Day by day, I was having fierce arguments with this group of young people about the existence of God, yet all the while, my jaw was dropping at the things I was seeing, and more especially, the joy and the laughter, and the gentle patience that they had for me as I attempted to batter and bruise them in their belief. It was something very special, and I had never experienced anything like it.

Bit by bit, I began to try to pray myself. They also gave me my first Bible, one of those small black ones with coloured pictures of the Holy Land every few chapters. Then one day, I was walking with Asaph in the woods, and he asked if I wanted to say a prayer with him. It would be one of those prayers where you invite Jesus into your heart and give your life to Him. I obliged Asaph, rather than embarrass him with a 'no', and so I repeated the words that he said, but I wasn't particularly engaged. I remember a cuckoo in the background somewhere in the forest and which distracted my attention while he was praying. Nonetheless, I said the words, but I didn't think then that it had meant much.

It was late August, and I didn't have long to work with Tom and Foster Associates in Oslo before returning to take up the next part of my studies. I had managed to arrange an exchange year at America's oldest technological research university, Rensselaer Polytechnic in Troy, upstate New York, and I was beginning to talk to Tom about some of the things I was experiencing with Heidi, Asaph, and the others. Tom thought I had gone completely nuts and was possibly a liability to the business and a potential embarrassment to his clients, and so, within a few days, I was fired. I only had a week before leaving anyway, so it was no big deal, but those few days off work gave me the opportunity to try to think about what I was supposed to be doing with my life. I was 22 years old and as far as I was concerned, I thought I had everything planned and arranged, and yet, I was becoming increasingly unsure.

I decided to take a whole day out and find a remote place in pine woods by the fjord where I could ask God what on earth I was supposed to be doing with my life. Should I go to the States as planned? Should I stay with my new friends in Norway? What should I do? I found a beautiful spot overlooking the water and sat there most of the day expecting something to happen. I didn't feel I had much of a connection with God and I didn't know what I was asking for, or even how to ask, but I knew I was trying to ask for something, anything. I wanted a sign, I suppose, some direction for my future, even though I'd had it all planned out just a few weeks before. I sat for hours, as long as I could, and then I thought it was probably a waste of time so, reluctantly, I got up to leave, disappointed at drawing a blank.

As I was leaving the water, I looked back through the trees still hoping for something. But nothing. Then I moved further on and looked a second time. Still nothing. By the time I looked a third time, the water I had been overlooking was nearly out of sight but could just be glimpsed through the pine trees where I had been. However, I could now see another part of the fjord about a quarter of a mile away. As I looked, a huge flock of seabirds rose up vertically from the nearside of the fjord.

There were hundreds and hundreds of them. I hadn't noticed them before and probably they hadn't been visible from where I had sat all day. They rose up together as one and then took a minute or two to fly across to the other side of the fjord and settle down on the water there. As they did so, I heard a clear voice. It was just one word. 'Go!' I knew I had my answer. I was to go across the water to America.

Because I'd been fired, I still had a few days before I needed to get back to London, to say goodbye to my parents in Cambridge and then continue arrangements for the States. Before leaving, I decided to visit Bergen and then to return to Oslo and catch a ferry down the Oslo Fjord and visit Copenhagen. There was also a house in Malmo in Sweden where my Oslo friends had said I could visit before going back to England. I had some funds because there was a huge differential in salaries between Norway and the UK and I think they had to pay me way above what I was getting in London. In fact, I had been incredibly lucky and had been paid more in Oslo than Norman Foster's more senior London Associates.

I spent a couple of days visiting Bergen and was about to embark on the first leg of the journey that would take me eventually to my year in the States. I had everything with me, money, passport, and tickets, and so I caught a bus to Bergen train station to begin my return. The bus was nearly empty as I sat down, and as I did so, I heard a voice again. It sounds crazy, but it broke across my thoughts and was completely clear and it said, 'You're going to lose your wallet.' My wallet contained everything, all my money and my documents. I didn't think to question the voice and I didn't think, 'That must be God', but I did respond. I very carefully put my wallet, with everything tucked in it, in my left-hand inside jacket pocket. I checked it, checked it again, and zipped it in and then folded my right arm across my jacket from the outside in order to press it close to my chest. I thought, 'There's no way I'm going to lose this wallet.'

The bus dropped me a little way from the station, and I didn't have long for the train to depart so I went straight to the ticket office and reached into my jacket pocket. It was gone! I couldn't believe it. I checked everywhere, but everything had gone.

I walked away from the ticket office wondering what on earth to do when it occurred to me that I might speak to God. I was suddenly questioning everything. What if I was mistaken about the sign I'd seen with the birds and the fjord, and the voice I'd heard saying 'Go!'? What if I was supposed to give up my career and stay with Heidi and 'Gud's Barn' in Oslo? I had been used to planning my future, and I had been growing more and more confident about how things might turn out as I planned ahead, but right then I had no idea what to do. Alone on the street and with no one in sight, I looked up to the sky and said, 'Lord, I will do whatever you want me to.' It seemed more than an appeal to get me out of a tight spot. I think I really meant it, though at the time I had no idea what was happening and no idea how significant that response would be for the rest of my life. On later reflection, they were probably some of the most important words I would ever say.

I was recounting all of this to Richard before drawing him back to the first lunch we had had after fishing.

"Richard, we spoke some time ago and you asked me, 'does God still speak?' Well, this is partly why I am telling you about some of my first experiences. I hadn't really learned to recognise God's voice, and, since those few occasions in Norway, I've barely heard Him speak to me in that same kind of way, audibly and intrusively without any hint that He was about to do so, and without me really recognising that it was His voice. But at that time, he was indeed speaking loud and clear. After I had looked up and said, 'Lord, I will do whatever you want me to,' He spoke that way again, though this time, I really knew it was His voice because I had just spoken to Him. He said quite simply, 'Go back the way you came.'

"Now, I thought that meant going back to Oslo, going back to Heidi and Asaph and the folk I had met. I thought it probably meant the end of my studies, my career as an architect, indeed, the end of everything that I thought had been laid out for me in life according to the way I had planned it. And so, I did start back, up the same road I had just come down to the station. It was a few hundred yards to a T-junction and as I reached it, a bus went past and then braked to stop. A little way down the road, the driver got out and ran over to me. He said, 'Your wallet is in the bus station,' and he pointed the direction and went back to the bus. I ran there as fast I could and sure enough, it had been found on the bus and handed in.

"My train should have left by then, and there weren't many trains a day between Bergen and Oslo, so I was hoping without much hope that there might have been a delay and ran back down to the station. By then, the ticket office was closed, and so was the gate to the platform, but I could see that the train was still there. A man was standing waiting at the platform entrance. He moved to unlock the gate onto the platform and said, 'Get on.' And so I did, without a ticket.

"I started later at the beginning of the autumn term at Rensselaer Polytechnic Institute in upstate New York. President Ford had just pardoned Nixon from the Watergate scandal and Harold Wilson was soon to become Prime Minister. He and his wife Mary were members of the Vineyard Church after the war when they lived on Richmond Green, though I knew nothing of that at the time."

Chapter 6.

Hearing Voices

Richard and I talked for quite a while on that first meeting in the garden and had listened at length to each other's stories before he began to pick up on some things I had said.

"Bob, in your present life, do you meet a lot of people who have had the same experience of a voice? You said you heard a voice say, 'Go,' and it was an actual voice, and then again in the bus and so on. Do you meet a lot of people who are blessed in that way? I would have thought it was quite unusual."

I tried to explain. "Well, it's not usual for me either, Richard, but it's not that unusual to hear of stories like that either. Yes, I have met many who hear God speak in that way. I don't mean 'hearing voices,' as in the kind of thing that many of us hear from time to time. You know, things that rattle around inexplicably in our head or interrupt us while half asleep, chatter and thought that is of no particular consequence.

"I have found that God speaks in many ways. For instance, God spoke to me through a vision once. I had a waking vision of the girl I was to marry the night after I first met her. She said in the vision, 'I love you.' I'll tell you about that sometime. But God does speak, in dreams and visions, through people, and particularly through the Bible. Sometimes He speaks audibly, like my experiences in Norway. I don't know how many times the Bible records various forms of 'God said', but it must be thousands, and just about every Bible character we know of hears God speak in one way or another. When you read the Bible expressions like 'God said', 'God spoke' or 'the word of the Lord came to so and so', these phrases run right through the Bible from beginning to end, Old Testament and New. In fact, I think God speaks right through the first chapter of the Bible, in Genesis. You barely get two lines in before you read 'God spoke.'

"Take what happened to the apostle Peter. I know we fishermen are prone to exaggeration, Richard, but Peter was a rough, hard-working open-air sort of guy who knew the difference between the sound of wind in his sail and the voice of God. When he was hungry and up on a rooftop praying one evening, he went into a sort of trance and had a vision of a sheet being lowered with all kinds of animals, reptiles and birds in it and he heard an audible voice say to him 'Get up, kill and eat.' It happened three times, but Peter was a good Jew and the animals he was being asked to eat were unclean ones and so he protested vigorously that he really shouldn't eat.

"Peter came out of this trance and hadn't a clue what this was all about but while he was puzzling over it, the Spirit spoke to him saying that there were some men coming from Caesarea and that he should go and answer the door. And the rest of the story unfolds as being one of the most important events in history when the news of the gospel of Jesus was first brought to the Gentiles.

"So, on that occasion, God 'spoke' in several ways. First, in a trance where Peter saw a vision, then in an audible voice that he could converse with, and also 'by the Spirit' who told him about the men who were looking for him. And these men had only come because an angel sent by God had spoken to their master Cornelius. So, we have a whole range of ways in which God was communicating in just those few paragraphs which tell that story, which itself is written as God speaking to us because all scripture claims to be God-breathed, inspired by God such that He speaks to us as we read. Yes, God speaks, Richard, and not just to the special people, but to the tax collectors, the shepherds, to women and young children, and to ordinary fishermen like Peter, and like you and me. People hear Him in different ways though. Some feel more at home in their conversation while out for a walk in the park, while others may be on their knees in their room or meditating on scripture. The point is that Jesus said His sheep hear His voice, and they know it, they recognise it, and they follow Him.

"When I was in Norway, I was only just beginning to recognise His voice, and I certainly knew nothing of the Bible. In those circumstances, I think God might sometimes speak in the way that we speak to little children. 'Stop! Don't cross the road! Time for bed!' When we grow up, we not only learn to recognise His voice, but we learn the kind of things He might and might not say. I think we learn to recognise His inner voice to us as well, one which is not so direct as audible words, or a vision. When we have got to know God's character and His ways, and how He guides us through the Bible to live our lives, then, for the most part, His communication changes from the audible interruptions which I first experienced. Many don't hear His voice audibly, yet they still learn to recognise when He speaks.

"I tend to think of it this way. As God teaches us, we can start to work in the family business without Dad always having to tell us exactly what to do and when to do it. We grow up from being young children and our father talks to us as beloved and trusted sons and daughters. He shouldn't have to shout if we know how to listen, and He shouldn't have to direct every action or answer every question if we have already learned what would please Him. If the guidance and encouragement of the Bible becomes part of our daily life then we don't need to ask, 'should I love my neighbour?'"

"I suppose I'm quite hung up on this hearing God's voice thing," Richard persisted. "There are bits of the Bible where a man, it might be Elijah or someone, is reporting what God has told him; what God says. I wonder how many people like me find that hard to take. I can understand that a solitary hermit, out in the desert or whatever, and fasting, enduring the harsh conditions, might well hallucinate, find Nirvana, and so on, and then hear voices, as a schizophrenic hears voices. When I think of mystics who are of other faiths, the received wisdom is that if you isolate yourself and practice abstinence for long enough, you stand a better chance of making contact with whatever the Almighty is. Do you ever meet or talk with mystics? Or is the analogy not valid?"

I didn't really know how to answer Richard. My own experiences were so far from being mystical in the way that people might imagine. I was a long way from some sort of transcendental journey, taking a trip to India to find myself, that sort of thing. On the other hand, my experiences had indeed been a mystery, and not so easy to explain or accept.

"That's probably a minefield, Richard. I think it's valid to the extent that Jesus said to his disciples, 'when you pray, when you fast....' In other words, there was an expectation that they should pray and fast. Jesus instructed them to go and do it in secret and not make a show of it. He tells us that our Father in heaven, who sees what is done secretly, will reward us. Yet, Jesus made no mystical secret of His instruction. He was plain-speaking, not mystical, even if they didn't at first understand Him or His parables.

"He seems very different from an Eastern mystic, for example. For a start, Eastern mystics are not often trying to commune with God, certainly not the creator God. Buddhists don't believe in a creator God anyway. My impression is that most Eastern mysticism is about escaping from this created world and its evil. For that kind of mysticism, creation is considered inherently inferior, even evil. That goal is about finding an altered state, like Nirvana, something transcendent, something above it all.

"And it's so often a self-help transformation that they are looking for, something to do with their own efforts in holiness, fasting, prayer or whatever, rather than a recognition that we need God's help, that we cannot find God unless He enables us. Mystics see Jesus, Buddha, Krishna, and others they regard as 'gurus', as all teaching the same thing; find the path of enlightenment through your own efforts of self-righteousness. But that's not the Christian faith. God loves all of His creation, and its design is not inherently evil. When He created mankind, He saw what He had made was good, and mankind was 'very good'. But it's gone bad, Richard. It needs a fix which is not a self-help one; it's not something that we can fix ourselves, nor is it escapism."

"But were you not in an altered state when you sat beside the fjord?" Richard asked. "I mean, you sat there for a whole day. You see what I'm getting at? Some sort of transcendental experience?"

I laughed. "Richard, in all honesty, I was pretty bored and uncomfortable, certainly not into some kind of ecstatic transcendental experience. It was very ordinary, sitting on a cold hard rock, feeling hungry, and with my mind wandering here and there thinking about lunch and then supper, the smell of the pine trees, and girls, especially thinking about girls, and a thousand other random thoughts between checking my watch for the time. It was a long way from a mystical ecstasy. I nearly got up to leave several times!

"I'll grant you that the Christian faith is full of mystery, though. There is a great mystery about God, but that's not the same as the New Age kind of stuff. The God of the Bible has history, clarity, and certainty. If we want to know and understand the mystery of God and what He is like, then we should look at Jesus who reveals God in Himself. John's gospel points to that mystery of God in His first words, 'In the beginning was the Word, and the Word was with God, and the Word was God'... Richard was familiar with that scripture and joined in with the last part of my quotation. "That's all pretty mysterious, isn't it? Until fourteen lines into that first chapter, we read that the Word became flesh and dwelt among us. God became a human being, made of the same stuff as you and me, and He made His home amongst us as Jesus Christ. At a certain time and place, God revealed Himself, and it was precisely because Jesus claimed to be the unknowable God who had come down from heaven to make

Himself known, taking the titles of the Son of God and Son of Man, that He was rejected and put to death. Not for nothing did Jesus say, 'he who looks at me is seeing the one who sent me.' Jesus is God revealed in flesh and blood, who ate and drank, grew tired like us and bled like us, and yet revealed in Himself the great mystery of the same person who created the universe.

"The Gnostics tried to give credibility to a false mystical view of Jesus not long after the New Testament events. One of the characteristics of Gnosticism was the development of so-called special, esoteric knowledge, something that was secret, hidden. I think that's the root of the meaning of mystic, something that is mysterious and not revealed. That kind of teaching is about being 'in the know.' If you are one of the chosen ones in the secret club, it will lead to salvation, union with the absolute, or whatever.

"But the 'Jesus' described by those false gnostic gospels didn't come in person. The so-called gnostic Jesus was not thought of as flesh and blood like the biblical Jesus. John the apostle wrote about those heresies calling those who perpetrated them anti-Christs. He was so keen to counter that mystical corruption of the plain truth that he wrote about it at the very beginning of his gospel, and again several times in his letters. Let me find something for you."

I opened my phone Bible and clicked to the first chapter of John's first epistle and then read a little to Richard from the first verse: 'That which was from the beginning, which we have heard, which we have seen with our eyes, which we have looked at and our hands have touched – this we proclaim concerning the Word of life. The life appeared; we have seen it and testify to it, and we proclaim to you the eternal life, which was with the Father and has appeared to us.'

"It's pretty clear that John is saying that the flesh and blood they touched, who was also the Word in the beginning, the Life that was with God and was God in the beginning, that was the same Jesus in front of them that they saw and touched. The mystery of the eternal Word with God appeared as flesh and blood to live with them. They did not transcend to try and find the mystical absolute. Rather, God came down to live with them as a human being; Jesus, a baby in a manger, a carpenter, a man who was put to death on a cross alongside two criminals.

"The Da Vinci Code and all that stuff about Mary Magdalene, and the Illuminati, the secret 'enlightened' society, it's just a revival of all that mystical gnostic heresy. People love it; they love a mysterious and secret knowledge which gives a certain power to those who claim to understand it, the special people, but Jesus said that what he had done and spoken, He did openly and not in secret. And Paul wrote much the same to the Corinthian church saying that the truth was set out plainly, not with deception or distortion or secret and shameful ways.

"Richard, the Christian faith I have come to know isn't about mystical knowledge. It *is* about union with what you might call the absolute, or what some call a higher power, or if you're a Star Wars fan it would be the Force, but that relationship is not vague and intangible, it is with a very real and knowable person; the same God who is revealed in Jesus, and the same Jesus who is alive today and with us by His Spirit. And when he speaks it isn't the same as studying a guru's sayings or getting a bit of information from Alexa. His words are creative, transformative, and powerful, whether it was simply 'Quiet! Be still!', and the storm on Lake Galilee calmed immediately, or the even greater mystery of how God spoke the heavens and the earth into being. So, when God speaks, Richard, just one word is enough to change our lives."

"That all needs a bit of what I call cosmic thinking," Richard replied. "I mean, this is clearly not about the power of the voice box, but now that you mention it, I do recollect something in the Psalms about God refusing to be silent. Did I remember that right?"

I searched my phone Bible and thought maybe he was recollecting the beginning of Psalm 50. "Is this it, Richard?"

'The Mighty One, God, the Lord, speaks and summons the earth from the rising of the sun to where it sets. From Zion, perfect in beauty, God shines forth. Our God comes and will not be silent...'

"And something else comes to mind from the beginning of the book of Hebrews: 'The Son is the radiance of God's glory and the exact representation of His being, sustaining all things by His powerful word.' [1] You're right, Richard. This is indeed cosmic, and clearly not something to be equated with the human voice box."

---

[1] Hebrews 1:3

Chapter 7.

Parallel Universes with Wormholes

Ashmere Lakes operate a closed season for August and September, but I continued to meet Richard at various coffee bars and occasionally for a lunch or a walk. It didn't always work out as we both had some trouble with e-mail, and he didn't always pick up his mobile, but mostly we could hook up for an hour or two each week. I was keen to know where his faith stood and what he believed. I thought that I would have to let him be comfortable in our honesty, but it wasn't long before a walk down to the Thames gave an opportunity to ask a question as we had coffee at Tide Tables under Richmond Bridge.

"Richard, I'd love to know about your faith. I know you go to St. Mary's Church now, and we have spoken before that this 'pilgrimage' is as much a spiritual journey for us as it is exploring lives and stories about fishing."

Richard drew breath and responded. "You'll have gained the correct impression by now, Bob, that I'm a somewhat superficial person. I sort of float along and rely a lot on being, you use the word favoured, I use the word lucky. Just outside Chelmsford, there was then a village called Springfield; it's part of the town now. It was quite a small village with a lovely, lovely village church, a green and a pond. And that's where I was born. My grandparents on my mother's side were church-going. I don't think my father's parents in Penzance were, but they led respectable lives.

"We all went to the parish church. It wasn't a question of religion then; we all did it. It was a natural part of village life. I quite like that aspect of Christianity, a welding together of community and not actually asking a lot of questions but leading ordinary good lives. When I was six, I joined the choir until my voice broke at twelve. I became the head choirboy. Right now, if you ask me, I can remember all the breaks and stresses of the psalms. It's called pointing, and I can still do all of that in my head. So, what am I saying? There's a sort of bedrock of memory still there, training I suppose, and a culture of the age. Then, when my voice broke, I wanted to go on to be a tenor, but I didn't have a tenor voice, so I took up bellringing until I left home.

"At school, we had assembly and hymns every morning but when I left school in '49, I had a year of drifting, I suppose, and then I didn't go to church. I was out and about with two or three boys, on bikes, going swimming and that sort of thing, and I worked as a ward orderly at a local hospital. When I started medicine at 19, I think it's true to say that I was not then a practising Christian for many years. I qualified after medical studies and did a house job, like your year-out as an architect. That was at a surgery at St Peter's Hospital in Chertsey, and by the end of 12 months, you are supposed to be safe enough to be let loose on the public. That's an act of faith in itself!

"One of the things I think back on is that a lot of the time we were dealing with people who were extremely ill, and surgery might or might not have done the trick. And when you are at someone's bedside at the moment they die, which I often was because the sister would call me, you have this thing when, at one moment, you have a sentient being, with a brain, a mass of jelly that is miraculously full of memory. I mean, if I asked you to sing me a song that you learnt when you were eight, I bet you could sing it. So, one moment you have a sentient human being, and perhaps you have spoken to them a moment before, and then they are not there. I found that very hard to deal with, not in the sense that it frightened me or upset me but in the sense of 'What the hell's going on here?' And I've never answered that question.

"Except that I have times, thinking about all this, when I think one of the answers that might work is the idea of a parallel universe. A parallel universe with wormholes. There are people who will talk to you about this and it's quite convincing. What about all that stuff inside here, the mind, where does all that stuff go? I think about it a lot, but I have no answers."

Chapter 8.

Drawing Near to Kiss

Parallel Universe! That was a surprise. That the village-choirboy-senior-medic, now retired and in his eighties, would be into parallel universe theory. Mind you, I knew that scientists were increasingly more fascinated by the possibilities. In a sense, Richard was right. The Bible is clear that there *is* a kind of parallel universe. There is the seen world and the unseen world, both equally real, a natural dimension and a spiritual one. The spiritual dimension is inhabited by disembodied spiritual beings, including God and the angels, and the natural world is something we all know about, but humanity is unique and unlike angels has both spirit and decaying bodies.

Richard had paused and I wondered if I should jump in and tell him of all the glorious certainties of the Christian faith, the resurrection of the dead and the promises of eternal life, in glorious spiritual bodies that no longer sin or suffer. I felt that I knew about so many of the Bible's answers to his questioning, but I also wondered if it was possible for him to understand or accept them just yet. We finished our coffee and took a walk in the sunshine along the towpath, and Richard continued where we had left off.

"When I was a house doctor at St. George's, I had a lot of patients on my ward who were coughing up what I would call cupfuls of custard! I was still seeing men who had been gassed in the First World War. They didn't have much of a life and you did what you could for them. I think what happened was, that looking back on it, I felt that being a doctor and doing what I did was probably enough. Arrogance, I suppose."

"Enough for what?" I asked. "To feel that I was living a good life," Richard replied. We walked on in silence for a moment enjoying the sunshine. "Richard, I didn't tell you about what happened on the way back to London from Norway. You remember that my friends had suggested I drop into a house in Malmo which they were connected with? I decided to do that. By then, I was beginning to pray a bit and stumble through a few pages of the Bible, but really the big draw was the human companionship and the love that I was receiving from these young people. I honestly don't think that if someone had asked me at that point whether I was a Christian, or really knew God's personal love for me, I could have answered with any certainty.

"There was a young girl in the Malmo house with a newborn baby. I understand now that she was probably tired, and her hormones might have been a bit all over the place, but I hadn't a clue about those things then, so I made the mistake of entering a closed door to a room where she was breastfeeding. She chewed me out quite abruptly and I retreated. I was alone in the adjacent room, so I put my head down and sort of began to reflect and I suppose to pray, though not about anything in particular. When I say 'pray', I didn't really know much about that then, but I was being drawn to try and talk to God and I was certainly aware that something was stirring within me.

"It was at that time of attempted prayer that I really became aware of God's presence for the first time. I mean, His presence with me, as opposed to that voice which had barged in from somewhere out there. It's hard to describe, but I became intensely aware of a presence, of being in His presence, of somehow entering into a place that was profound and glorious. "Whilst I was wrapped up in this, I became aware of the door opening into the room and the young mother coming out. As she walked past the sofa behind me, not wanting to disturb me no doubt, she just planted a gentle kiss on the back of my head. She had given just a little sign that she forgave me; she forgave my insensitivity and my indiscretion with her need for privacy while breastfeeding. It was a small thing, a simple reconciliation.

"But what happened in the physical was being mirrored far more profoundly in the spiritual, and without my attention being diverted to the girl, I knew then for the first time that God had forgiven me too. While I had been praying, I had experienced a profound heaviness. Not a depressive heaviness or anything like that, but I had felt a great weight upon my soul and when I received that human kiss of forgiveness, and the Lord's assurance of His forgiveness for me at the same time, the heaviness was replaced by a great joy flooding in. When those minutes had passed, I was a changed person, and I knew it.

"Something happened in the unseen spiritual world that was mirrored in our physical world. When we have a bust-up with someone, particularly someone we love, there is the wounding of a broken relationship. It really hurts, and if there is no reconciliation, we just have to mask our hurt and get on with life until our sensitivities subside. But the damage is done and is still there unless there is an apology, forgiveness, and a restoring of the relationship. If we stay unreconciled then our hearts are wounded, less trusting, more guarded, less free. But if there is forgiveness and reconciliation, along with the restoration of love and honest communication, then a weight is lifted, and we find the freedom to breathe in joy again.

"We start life with a busted relationship with God, Richard, and that's our fault, not His. It's our wilfulness, ignorance, rebellion, and unbelief that separate us from the close relationship that he longs for, and that we are often ignorant of, though deep down we know there is something missing, and we suffer. God never intended that we should live our lives separated from Him. When my head was down in prayer on that sofa, the weight of all that fractured relationship was lifted. I knew I was forgiven, and I experienced the joy of God's love flooding in.

"I have learned since that the biblical words used for worship mean 'drawing near to kiss.' And there is a bit in Psalm 2, a messianic Psalm speaking of Jesus, which says, 'kiss the Son lest He be angry with you'. How ironic that Jesus was also betrayed by a kiss. It's not a physical act I'm talking about, which can obviously be counterfeit, like Judas' kiss; it's the touching of spirits. I learned later that what was probably happening to me in Malmo was that my spirit was being kissed by the Holy Spirit. There was restored communion with God.

"I have also since learned that something probably happened to me which the Bible describes as being 'born again.' You can read about that in chapter three of John's gospel, and I'm sure we'll explore it sometime, though, at that encounter in Malmo, I had little understanding of what that was about, not until some years later.

"Now, bear in mind, Richard, that I had experienced absolutely nothing of church or Christianity up to the point when Heidi came and spoke to me in Oslo. From the age of seven, our home was in a short cul-de-sac road in Cambridge. As kids, we played in the street most days after school and in holidays, with carts and bikes and that sort of thing, and amused ourselves by doing silly stunts like seeing how far we could cycle down the road with our eyes closed. There was no traffic then, but I remember Mr Baker's new Morris Minor parked outside his house didn't do too well with that game.

"Roller skating was all the rage and there was a lovely, paved forecourt of a church at the top of the road, St. George's C. of E., I think. We used to roller skate on it until we were chased off by someone; I suppose it was the vicar, or maybe it was the verger. I ventured inside the open door of the church once and it was dark and dingy and generally not a welcoming place, and, since my parents were atheists, I really had no experience of church or faith at all, unlike you and your upbringing in Springfield.

"I knew for certain that my R.E. teacher at grammar school didn't believe in God because he liked to tell us so. That was crazy, really, a bit like the history teacher saying he didn't believe that Julius Caesar or Henry the VIII existed. So, it's no surprise that I didn't have any experience of God or Christianity or church until what I talked to you about in Norway, and then it wasn't at all like church in the way you knew it, Richard. I didn't go to church or even know what church was. But in Norway, and after, I did have plenty of experiences of God."

Chapter 9.

The Mystery of the Universe

I thought I would tell Richard about one of those experiences I had just after I had joined my first church, about five years on from Norway. It was a young and vibrant congregation who met in a borrowed Anglican church in Earl's Court, and later it was where I was to meet my wife. For some reason that I don't quite remember now, I had to fly to the States again. As a fledgling architect, I had a commission to build a ski house in Vermont but the only thing I can now recall about that trip is the flight out. By then, I had begun to understand a bit about the Bible and become pretty active in my faith, a bit of an evangelist if you like, and probably a pretty annoying one to complete strangers. I had laid out this background to Richard and then continued with what happened.

"When I was in the departure lounge and looking around at fellow passengers, I noticed quite a number who were obviously from different religions. There were a couple of orthodox Jews with their sidelocks and black fedora hats. Also, some men in black robes whom I took to be Muslims. I noticed a brown-robed Capuchin monk and a couple of young eastern 'devotees' in orange robes, maybe Buddhists.

"I thought, 'Wow!' and I wondered who I might sit next to and perhaps have the chance of a good conversation as we travelled across the Atlantic. I couldn't wait to find out and I was reminding the Lord in idle chatter with Him that this was His opportunity to pass the ball, so to speak, so that I could score. I boarded what was obviously going to be a pretty full plane and was on board quite early and settled by a window with two empty seats next to me. The plane filled up, and filled up some more, and luggage lockers were getting closed, and the cabin doors locked, and no one had come to sit next to me. I stood up in my seat to look around and the *only* seats empty were the two right next to me.

"I was more than a little cross and disappointed. I said something to the effect: 'Lord, what are you playing at? Don't you know that I could be winning hearts and minds for you here? I thought I would have an open goal for at least five hours. Why didn't you pass the ball?' I know most people would be absolutely delighted to have two empty seats next to them for a long-haul flight but at that time, for me, it felt as though I had been red-carded and confined to the bench. I had a good old grumble and a sulk whilst we waited to take off.

"It was a really grey and miserable winter day at the airport. The Heathrow landscape was thoroughly depressing as I looked out of the window, and we taxied for take-off. But you've flown a bit and you must have experienced this, Richard. There's a moment at some point, soon after take-off, when you break through that blanket cloud cover and suddenly the heavens are before you; deep blue clear skies stretching to infinity.

"When I was gazing up at the blue heavens, that's when the Lord spoke. It was a clear, clear voice, but not quite the same as the audible ones I had heard before. It was somehow nearer, inside me, and it was so far from what I was thinking, so tender and yet so shocking to me in its content, that I was immediately and deeply impacted, completely poleaxed by the preposterous words that I heard.

"As I looked out of the window, God said, 'I made all of this for you.' And then after a slight pause, He said, 'and to you, I have revealed the mystery of the Universe.'

"Straight away, I burst into tears. I knew it was God speaking and my immediate and overwhelming reaction was, 'Lord, you can't say that to me! You can't possibly say that to *me*.' I thought, 'those words are too impossible for anyone to receive from the Creator of the Universe'. Of course, I knew that God created the Universe for His pleasure and for the whole of mankind, certainly not just me, but in that moment, His words were spoken quite directly and very gently just to me. Their meaning was so far beyond comprehension in extravagance and grace that I could not comprehend or receive them, but they went straight to my heart and impacted my emotions."

"And you're weeping now," Richard said, after I paused for a while trying to stay composed. I was beginning to choke up, as I often do when I recount this, or remember God's extravagant goodness in so many ways. I continued talking to Richard with some difficulty.

"It was so outrageously gracious, Richard, and I really didn't know what God was saying, but I felt that I couldn't bear it. I wept and wept buckets. I wept for the whole five hours across the Atlantic. The cabin crew got so concerned that various members would come and check on me every half hour or so. But I would just nod to their questions, 'I'm OK, I'm OK,' and I kept my face looking out to the sky. As it turned out, I was so glad that I had empty seats next to me!

"I don't think at that time that I could grasp what God was saying. I'm not sure that it was really about the words anyway. Perhaps they were more a vehicle to convey His love in such a way that something much deeper was transacted. But I know that it's no coincidence that God spoke those words to me when I was expecting to do a bit of 'work' for Him. I think that I reacted then a bit like Peter when he had toiled hard at fishing. Peter and his companions had worked all night and caught nothing when Jesus came along and said, 'Move into deep water and throw the net on the right side of the boat.' I can imagine what the expert fisherman Peter and his crew were silently thinking. The sun's up, we fished at the best time, there are no fish about, and you, Jesus, want us to try where we have just spent all night with no luck. But they did try again and caught such a huge catch of large fish that they began to sink. When Peter saw it, he fell at Jesus' feet and said, 'Go away from me, Lord; I am a sinful man!'

"When we see how big and how awesome God is, yet He cares for us intimately and personally, then I think, like Peter, we become aware that we are just not that great ourselves. We are not the one who knows how to draw the fish into the net or who can convert our fellow travellers across the Atlantic or score any goal of any kind through our own fancy footwork. In the midst of all of God's preposterous kindness, he gently draws us to our knees, and we can only look up and give thanks and worship. It then becomes hard to say that we think we are living a good life because we have done this, or we have done that, and that God should be happy enough with our offering. Love isn't impressed by what it gets in return. Love simply loves, and somehow God loves me, and He loves you.

"Richard, I have come to realise that God is not at all impressed by what we may have done, but He is transfixed in love by who we are, even that part of His creation which He saw was very good and yet which has rebelled and rejected Him so profoundly, crucified Him, put Him to death along with criminals even. In spite of that, He is now looking for those who want to draw near to kiss, who want to know His pardon and be reconciled to His love.

"I felt like that, Richard. I had been rolling my eyes at the Lord, giving instruction to Him on what He should do with the seats next to me, and yet He was revealing the awe and majesty of His creation. You see, Richard, I think when we come face to face with God's holiness, that He really is almighty God who spoke and created the heavens, yet He is so outrageously generous in creating such blessing for us, and when He fills Peter's boat with fish, and not with tiddlers either, and when He places someone like me at the centre of His grace, someone so completely unworthy of any of His love and attention at all, then we feel that He had better leave us alone because we are indeed sinful."

Chapter 10.

Bad News, Good News

We had met quite a few times by now and our conversations had gone in all sorts of directions. I don't think either of us felt guarded, and certainly, nothing was off-limits. We had nothing to prove, and it was rare for me to have an easy companion to talk with without any role to play except to explore conversation and friendship. We both listened thoughtfully to each other and there was never a change of subject if something might be awkward.

"Bob, I'm beginning to think that this is bad news. You heard me say that I thought I might have been 'doing enough', and I think I threw in an off-the-cuff comment, something like 'arrogant', I expect, but now I'm beginning to think that might really apply. Are you saying that God might not be much impressed by my 'doing enough'?"

We both laughed. "Richard, it is bad news - and extremely good news. It means that no matter what our earthly circumstances, and let's face it, you and I have both had pretty good ones compared to many, we all have the same grace to call on. No one can claim special privilege or qualification, no matter what our culture, our background, our race, nationality, or education. In time past or time to come, all mankind finds themselves in the same boat, and it turns out it's not a lifeboat but one that's sinking, and no one knows how to swim.

"Everyone is born separated from our God, who is holy, because of this sinful rebellion, sometimes ignorant, sometimes not, but no amount of doing enough is going to fix it, any more than a good deed done to your neighbour on the one side cancels the penalty for thieving from the one on the other. There is a penalty for breaking the law and there is a penalty for sin. That is a broken relationship with God, and the further consequence of that is death and hell. We can't fix it ourselves, and if we try to, there's a brass ceiling. Heaven is shut, not because God doesn't want us to commune, but because light and dark simply don't mix and any attempt to drag our own darkness into God's light meets with shutters drawn.

"That's the bad news, Richard, but the good news, the gospel, which is simply a word which means good news, is that God has reached down in love and opened a way to put that right. I mentioned before that the third chapter of John says that 'God so loved the world'. Well, He loves us and did something about our hopeless situation by giving us Jesus. God not only loved the world, but He gave His only begotten Son, He gave us Jesus so that anyone who believes in Him won't perish in our sin but rather have His gift of eternal life. Jesus opens heaven for us, and He alone can reconcile us with the Father. He's the One, the only One, who God chose to put things right. His sacrificial death on a cross accomplished all of that, and much more."

"I am inclined to conclude, Bob, that there are many more people who could repeat my story than could repeat yours. You started with nothing, you know what I mean, and I started with a background of, what shall we call it, good living, and church, and I would like to think I was influenced by it throughout my life. I suspect there are many people like that?"

"Absolutely," I said, "and I meet many people who are God-fearing, in the sense that they believe that there is a God and would assume that they are good-living. They assume that God would accept them because of that. But don't you think that would be a gospel of *self*-righteousness, Richard? That would not be good news at all, having to rely on our own goodness, and of course, when we put that word 'self' in front of righteousness it doesn't sound so great. No one likes a self-righteous person, and God finds no pleasure in self-righteousness either. Jesus reserved His harshest words for those who didn't realise that they didn't measure up and desperately needed Him."

Richard quipped, "I'm beginning to feel sorry that I had this coffee with you now." We laughed again.

Chapter 11.

Before They Call, I Will Answer

There was a pause in our conversation, we had finished our coffee and were just enjoying the sun as it moved slowly round our table overlooking the river and the coming and going of boats and skiffs by Richmond Bridge. No doubt, Richard was pondering some thoughts before he took up our chat again with a question.

"I remember something Archbishop William Temple said. It was something like: 'When I pray, coincidences happen.' Have you ever heard that, Bob? You see, every time I go to church, I'm a great believer in votive candles. If I kneel in front and focus on a candle flame, it helps me to settle my fears and think about what I'm there for.

"I'm sure I'm not alone in having what's called a grasshopper mind. You know, you go into church, and you've just been on the phone to your lawyer and so on, but you've got to get in and pray for what you want. Not infrequently, I find that something good will happen. The only thing I would say is, I have to set that against the fact that, particularly in later life, I've had what I explained to you the other day. I said I'm lucky. Lots of good things happen to me. Has God got nothing to do with that?"

I told Richard about my Uncle Francois, the middle one of my father and his brothers, and who was married to Betty. They were childless, and when I went to visit briefly, not long after Betty died, my uncle told me that I would be in his will to inherit his estate, which by the time he reached 90, was a modest bungalow in Sidmouth.

Uncle Fluff, as he was known, because he couldn't pronounce Francois as a youngster, was nineteen years older than my father and was alive as a small boy when his uncle, Oncle Albert, was a pioneer aviator between 1908 and 1912, when his plane crashed and he died. Born just a few years before, Fluff could remember his death and also just remember Bleriot's cross-channel flight in July 1909. He had many mementos and telegrams from his Oncle Albert, one of which was a telegram to my grandfather Charles which simply said, 'flew 2 kilometres, phone the family.'

My older cousin Denise had become a first godchild for Uncle Fluff, followed by myself when I was born a few years later. We had both been appointed godchildren, and we had also both become Christians, Denise a little before me, and quite separately, and she had later become an Anglican lay reader in Somerset. We had both been praying for our uncle. Denise particularly had spent time talking with him, and I also sent him some audio recordings of the Bible in his last years.

At the age of 90, Uncle Fluff became a Christian and died not long after. He was the last of my father's brothers to die and at the funeral in Sidmouth, I remember hearing my father quietly say to himself,

'Au Revoir, mon brave.' He was sad at losing his last brother, but Denise and I knew that Fluff was with the Lord.

Remarkably, my cousin Denise and I were the main beneficiaries of Fluff's will, two Christians the beneficiary of a third, and who had all quite independently come to faith. Cousin Denise and I arranged to visit his bungalow in Woolbrook Road in Sidmouth and to sort through his belongings and mementos which were numerous and of considerable interest. Denise had also arranged estate agent viewings for the second day of our visit, with explicit instructions that we would be too busy sorting through stuff on the first day. Pretty much as soon as she and I had arrived at the bungalow, we thought we had better pray. We sat down together and said something like, 'Lord, we have a lot of stuff to get through and then tomorrow we need to try and sell the bungalow, so please help us sort it all out quickly.' We both had busy lives and taking days out to be executors of Uncle Fluff's estate was not easy for either of us.

Within a few minutes of praying, there was a knock at the door, which Denise answered. She was in conversation for a minute or two and then came back to say that someone had come to view the property. She had explained to the visitor that the agent wasn't coming and that we weren't taking viewings that day. Denise was mildly irritated at the agent's mistake in arranging a visitor and, returning indoors, asked me what I thought we should do with the untimely intrusion. I went out and greeted the man who had by then retreated to the front gate as though he might leave. I repeated what he had probably already heard from Denise and then, as I was looking at him, I said, 'do I know you?' His face looked familiar somehow.

Perhaps I had seen him on television or somewhere like that, but I couldn't think how he was so familiar. He explained that he had come down from Cambridge that morning and was looking for a retirement bungalow to be near his daughter. He thought he had got the time right to meet the agent that day. As we were chatting, I mentioned that I had lived in Cambridge and been at school there until I was 18. When I mentioned my name, he said he knew it, and before long we had identified each other. He was Mr Graham, my gym master at Cambridge Grammar School. And so, of course, I invited him in, and we retold the coincidence to Denise.

While we were chatting, there was another knock on the door which Denise again answered, this time to a slightly flustered young man, the estate agent, who apologised for being a bit late. I expect Denise gave him a flea in his ear for getting it all wrong, but they settled to talk at the opposite end of the living room whilst I was reminiscing with Mr Graham. We had continued in our separate conversations for quite a few minutes when I looked over and became aware that something was going on between Denise and the young man. The conversation had become intense, and I noticed that the young man was weeping.

A few minutes later, when he was more composed, they came over to join us. Denise explained that one of her best friends, who had lived in Cambridge, had been dying of cancer. A few days before our current rendezvous at the bungalow, this friend had come to visit her in Wincanton and had died in her arms. I don't know how Denise and the agent's conversation had connected about this, perhaps it was the common thread of Cambridge, but Denise had talked about this in their chatting at the other end of the room and through twists and turns of the conversation, the young agent had discovered that Denise's friend was, in fact, someone he knew. He had lived in Cambridge himself when he was young, had been fostered as a child, and had just discovered that Denise's friend was his former foster mother. He hadn't known that she had just died.

When all this unfolded between the four of us, and we finished mopping our eyes and staring at each other, Mr Graham suddenly exclaimed, 'I don't believe in God, but this must be God! I'll buy the bungalow!' And so he did, at the asking price, and making the promise of purchase before he'd even looked around.

A photo of the 1969 Cambridge Grammar first XV rugby team, with me sitting in the front row, now hangs in our hallway. Mr Graham sent it to me as soon as he got home from Sidmouth. I was telling Richard this story and then concluded my thoughts.

"When we pray to God in a relationship of faith, Richard, coincidences happen. I can't explain how God worked all this out. I don't know how Denise and I were chosen as Fluff's godchildren at our births before the three of us knew of any connection with God as later-life Christians. When we prayed that morning for help to sell the property, someone, and not just anyone, knocked on the door within a few minutes, yet our prayer was clearly long after Mr Graham had already decided to set out and visit.

"I don't know how all that works, Richard, but I do know that God hears prayer, and in ways which we can't explain. In Isaiah 65 it says, 'Before they call, I will answer; and while they are still speaking, I will hear.' I believe God can apply today's prayer to last week's circumstances. I could tell you a thousand answered prayers, not all as strangely 'coincidental' as this one, but I know God listens. Often,

He answers very clearly, and often He doesn't appear to, at least not with the result that we are asking for. But people tend not to pray, and they don't ask unless they are in such trouble that they feel forced to. But then, those prayers are often not offered as though to a trusted friend, with the confidence and faith that God is alongside to hear them, but rather to some unknown power out there who may or may not be listening. The mantra is often: 'if all else fails we should pray' rather than we should pray and come to trust that all else will not fail.

"You mentioned votive candles, Richard. I think they are wonderful if they help you connect with God. But I suppose I have found that a lot of people who pray, and many do, pray in fear. You mentioned something yourself about calming fears. We can certainly cast our cares on Jesus if we are fearful, but not many really know that we can freely knock on God's door and that when we do, He opens it with a smile and not a frown. In fact, many people of all sorts of religious persuasions think that God still needs to be appeased before we can even approach His grand and forbidding entrance with our heavenly petition.

"People often think that God is still angry, or at best indifferent concerning humanity; that perhaps, like my dad, He even hates humanity in the mass, except for a very few special and exceptional saints. He gets blamed for all the bad things that happen, 'acts of God' they are called. In ancient cultures, they were sacrificing their firstborn in order to try and appease that kind of a god, or more often, several gods, but the idea that God is remote, capricious, indifferent, unconcerned with our personal struggles and our suffering, and doesn't hear prayer when offered, that idea of God is still in the back of many people's minds. They believe that there is something or someone, and yet have failed to seek the only God who is good.

"God has every right to be angry with us, of course, but He isn't. Even as a Christian, knowing that God's righteous anger, which should be directed at me, had been placed on Jesus, and that His sacrifice for us was sufficient once and for all to open our path to heaven, - even though I have known this for more than forty years, it has still taken me all those years to know deep down that I live under God's smile, in God's favour. Not only are we completely forgiven, Richard, but we are His favourites, along with countless others who love Him.

"I'm not lucky, Richard. Luck is just something that comes with the toss of a coin, or perhaps not.

"The 'mystery' that God said to me He had revealed all those years ago on that plane ride is something openly revealed in the Bible. It wasn't about the vastness of the created universe, or something out there in the great unknown. No, it was something much closer to us, that God wants to make His home in our hearts through faith, to walk and talk and enjoy being with us just as He did with Adam and Eve in the garden, before doubt and fear and sin crept in. When it did, you may remember, Adam and Eve hid and were afraid and were ashamed.

"I have known for years that there's nothing special to commend me to God. I do understand that it's only the cross of Jesus which puts me right with God and that everything I have been given is an undeserved gift. But it has still taken a long time to believe that God wants to be close, intimate, that he enjoys being with me and looks for my blessing and my prosperity. Yes, I mess up, and boy, do I mess up sometimes, and yes, I'm acutely aware that sin still affects my body. But the changed me on the inside, the me that was born again and reconciled to God for the first time in Norway, that me wants to love and honour Jesus as best I possibly can. God knows that. I know He knows that, and so I am completely free to welcome His presence in me, without fear but just with the joy of knowing His acceptance and His love. I am as much His precious inheritance as He is mine.

"That mystery which God spoke about to me on that plane ride was that the God who created the universe wanted to live inside me, and all who embrace Him by faith, and this is His plan to continue the reconciliation of the world to Himself. It is truly a mystery in many ways, Richard, not least that as a small part of His plan He should use someone so completely inadequate as me."

Chapter 12.

I Nearly Kill Dad

Between travelling from Norway to America, I had managed a couple of weeks back home in Cambridge when I finished my time in Oslo. Telephone calls home were not that frequent, but I phoned ahead to say I was coming. My father answered the call and after a few pleasantries said, "Here's your mother." I think some fathers did that then. This was well before mobile phones, when there used to be just one dial telephone on a table near the front door, used cautiously because of cost. Dad always picked up the phone in case it was something important and then quickly passed it to Mum if it meant chatty conversation. That was Dad when he picked up my phone calls, though he didn't generally do that face to face when there was always a warm greeting and interest in conversation about what I had been doing.

When I arrived from Norway after a three-month absence, I was hugely excited at seeing both my parents and I'm sure they were looking forward to seeing me. I wanted to tell them of my experiences and specially to tell them about my encounter with Jesus. They, on the other hand, were hoping to hear about my huge success as an architect. I hadn't yet told them I had been fired, something no doubt very significant for them and their hopes and expectations for me, but of little interest to me, and so straight after supper, I sat down with Dad intent on talking about Jesus and my experiences with Heidi and her friends. My mother ran out of the room when religion was mentioned but once Dad was in his usual armchair, and I had blocked him in by drawing up a stool, he had no escape.

Unfortunately, up to that point, I had just read bits and pieces of the Bible, pretty much unconnected and not entirely understood. I didn't know it well at all and I certainly didn't have any prior reference with my father for such a personal and challenging conversation. We had never talked about faith, belief, or any matters of real import. I started by picking out bits of scripture and throwing them like so many wooden balls at a coconut shy, expecting that sooner or later something would connect with my dad, and I would win the prize.

One of the scriptures was Luke 14.26, 'If anyone comes to me and does not hate father and mother, wife and children, brothers and sisters--yes, even their own life--such a person cannot be my disciple.' What on earth was I thinking! I didn't then understand the meaning and type of hyperbolic language being used, or the context, and much less so my father. He thought I had joined some cult, which to be fair, 'Gud's Barn', the Children of God, did later become. My conversation, if you could call it that, left him hugely perplexed and stressed.

The next day, Dad had a heart attack. He was barely 50 years old, and he never returned to work again. I thought I had nearly killed him, and so did my mother. From that day on she barely spoke to me for two years. She made arrangements for the vicar of the local church to 'sort me out.' That church was on the main road at the bottom of our street and the manse happened to be the house next door. My parents had never set foot in church but obviously knew the family next door to a degree and were certainly aware that he was the vicar. I can't otherwise imagine that they would have sought out a man of the cloth to intervene and 'put me straight', as it was conveyed to me. Mother had no idea that, in complying with her request to meet the vicar, he and I prayed together for my parents. It was the only time I met him, and I didn't stay long, but it turned out that there were unimagined outcomes of my unwise enthusiasm, of which one may well have been that the extra stress I had given my dad at that point in his life probably saved him. It seems likely that this early heart attack acted as a pressure release for what might have been much worse later on.

Dad had several more attacks over the years but survived them all. He had been a heavy smoker but stopped immediately. His last cigarette was that day I had come home. Although I was an enthusiastic idiot in my newfound faith, my being an idiot may well have saved his life.

Chapter 13.

Wanting to Be Loved

The Thames tide had slowed while we were talking, and the sun had moved around a little more so that we were shaded by one of the great big London plane trees near the towpath. We took a walk beside the Thames path towards Petersham and thought we could both head back through the Terrace Gardens, in my direction to the Vineyard and his a little further on to home. Richard had told me some of his early experiences about church, being a choirboy and so on, and I mentioned some of mine.

"In the cul-de-sac in Cambridge where we had that unwelcoming church at the far end, Richard, our house was the last at the bottom of the road and next door to us our only neighbour was an extremely grumpy lady and her husband. They were a childless couple, Mr & Mrs Reagan, or Raygun as we called them because their eyes beamed laser-like through their front bay window fixing on any child that dared move in the street. If we so much as walked on the patch of municipal grass directly outside their front fence, the net curtains were likely to twitch and there would be a rapid banging on the window. It could even result in the police being called if we stuck our tongues out. In those days, the police actually came for such a trivial complaint, and we were quite likely to get a dressing down for annoying an adult.

"If my father cut the hedge in our back garden and, if even the slightest clipping fell on their side, we would see it flying back again within a few minutes. Mrs Reagan particularly seemed to spend half her life skulking up and down on her side of the fence, silent and invisible, but we knew she was there whenever we went into our garden. There were one or two holes in the fence, knots that had fallen out, and bits of newspaper or tissue had been stuffed in each one from their side. If we were in the garden and tweaked a piece of tissue out it would be replaced almost instantly by another one stuffed back in. I think it was particularly Mrs Reagan who must have been lurking and watching and waiting for us to put the slightest foot wrong, though she never once spoke to us.

"I think some people still think God is like that, Richard; that He lurks with a big frown and can't wait to catch us out and throw back any rubbish that falls on his side of the fence, even if we try our best not to let it.

"The prodigal son in Luke 15 was also fearful of his father's reaction. He knew he'd blown it big time by demanding his inheritance and then squandering it on wild living. He didn't expect a welcome back from his father. When he came back home, he thought he'd be rejected by the family and have to work like a hired hand and pay off his debt. But instead, the father in Jesus' story is longing for his lost son to return and can't wait to see him again. It seems from the parable that the father has been scanning the horizon every day since his son's departure. When at last he appears, this

Middle Eastern father abandons all dignity, hitches his robe up and runs to greet his lost son, casts himself to embrace him with a kiss on his neck, places a new ring on his finger to restore his family status, and places the sandals on his feet that are used for the honoured guest. There is a great celebration party at the son's return and the best fatted calf is served.

"There is an older brother too, Richard, it's not just the one son. This older son is scandalised at the gracious welcome for this 'no-good son of his father', and he is very angry that such favour has been shown to this squandering and profligate brother. He accuses his father of never having done anything for him. He thinks he has lived a good life, worked hard in the fields, and that he is the one who has surely done enough to deserve the father's honour and favour. But we see from the father's reply that this older son also had access to everything and could have come in to enjoy the party for the one who was lost and dead but is now found and alive. But the older son refuses the invitation to celebrate with the father.

"God doesn't turn anyone away, Richard, and especially those who really know their need. But many are too fearful to draw close, or too self-righteous to accept the invitation. God's grace and favour is an affront to this kind of self-righteous pride. It's not just your arrogance, Richard; you mentioned it a while back, that you may have been arrogant in your thoughts of being good enough; it's the pride of all of us that keeps us at a distance. We think we can live our lives without God, that our best efforts are surely good enough. We are all older brothers, Richard, but unless we become like the younger one, we miss out on the welcome and the inheritance that is, in fact, graciously offered to both.

"Richard, you remember when I talked about that plane journey; I said that God chose to reveal His extravagant grace just at the time I thought I was doing my bit for Him, working hard in the field like the older brother in the prodigal story, I suppose. I think when I was at school and at university, I worked hard. And probably, like you, I was not bad academically. I was praised a lot at school by my parents who were proud that I was doing well, and why not? Every parent is proud of children who do well, and I think many live vicariously through their children's success. But this unwittingly reinforced the sense that my worth was through what I could achieve. I think that there are some good aspects of that kind of pride, pride in doing things well, but there is also a trap if it bolsters esteem through achievement instead of a person's innate value.

"Do you know that old Jewish joke? A Jewish mother on the beach sees her son getting into difficulty in the water and stands up to shout to everyone: 'help, help, my son, *the lawyer*, is drowning!' I think bit by bit, and quite unintended or recognised, that sense of achievement-equals- value, that set me on a path of being a bit of a workaholic. Deep down, my soul was gaining its worth through what I did, and not who I was. But, as I now know, I only flourish and I am only made whole by being loved as I am."

"I do know what you mean, Bob. We talked about prayer, and I didn't say it then, but I realise that I spend quite a bit of time apologising when I pray. I am mostly apologising because I'm aware that my faith is superficial. And I pray that it wouldn't be. You've picked it up before that I'm aware that I can be quite deferential, and I suppose what I'm saying is that I know that I have something formed in my character, and I'm not sure that it's particularly good.

I think it's probably some form of wanting to be loved. You know, you're sort of looking for approval. I don't think my being deferential and always apologising for myself is anything terrific, let's put it like that.

"I was recently having coffee with a chap in Richmond who lived next door to me when I was 12 and I used to babysit him when he was a baby. We were talking, and I knew that he had had a difficult marriage, and all of us who knew about it thought that he had cut himself off. I had been speaking to him for some time when I said, "I wonder, perhaps, possibly, do you think you could maybe tell me a bit about it? If you want to…." Something like that. And he wondered why I would go all round the houses before getting to the point. Why wouldn't I just come out with it?

"I thought that was typical of me, and I do tend to put things in terms of 'perhaps, I wonder if', that sort of thing, and I don't know why I do it, but it doesn't seem very good. Is it the fear of being rebuffed, you know, rejected in some way? You've picked it up. I think about it sometimes. In fact, I was thinking about it this morning before coming here. It says something about an insecurity in me, doesn't it? Yet I had a happy childhood. But these are very personal things; I don't think they're that important, are they?"

"I think it's probably very important, Richard. I had a happy childhood too. But I had a childhood probably devoid of much emotional affection."

"Not me," said Richard. "When I go to church now, the first thing I do is get down on my knees and give thanks for my parents because they sacrificed a lot to bring up the three kids who all turned out pretty good. My mother and father were very loving. I have nothing there to complain about."

"Richard, I have nothing to complain about either. My parents looked after us well, they cherished us, though I mentioned before that my parents probably received little emotional affection from their parents, and I think to that extent they found it difficult to give it to us boys, except as I said, to affirm our achievements, or convey disappointment.

"I think that was probably particularly difficult for my older brother because he wasn't quite so gifted academically, and then, without meaning to, parents can be setting up a sense of favouritism. That favouritism, and its subsequent damage, and the constant need to compete, I mean, compete with each other in such a way that we appear superior in order to feel good about ourselves, that part of our fallen nature is laid out very poignantly in Bible characters. Characters like Jacob and Joseph, for example. Even Peter, James and John struggled with competitive favouritism. They wanted to be favoured ahead of others rather than just favoured. It's quite a challenge, isn't it? To humble ourselves and consider others more important in the way that the Bible encourages us, and yet to find our esteem through the knowledge of God-esteem rather than self-esteem.

"I think that what I might be suggesting is that regardless of our backgrounds, everyone, every human being, needs to feel valued, significant and loved for their own sake. What happens is that the world values us for some other reason. It could be wealth, good looks, sporting prowess, as a consultant doctor, a budding architect, you name it, the list goes on and on. Now we live in an age where young people especially seem plagued with insecure identity, pursuing a 'me' culture of fame, fortune, and influence because they haven't found their true identity, that of a beloved child of God.

"I believe that for everyone there is a God-shaped hole. When I was younger, I looked for affirmation through something that can never fit or fill that hole. For me, it was probably focused on achievement, work, and also sex. I certainly wanted intimacy with the opposite sex. Not money. I don't think I was particularly interested in money, and not fame either. I think that's a phenomenon for younger people who have been wrongly taught that they can be whatever they want. I was receiving a sense of recognition through achievement, and because my sense of worth was constantly affirmed through intellect, and academic success, I thought that this was becoming the maturity of my soul. But I had no idea that this was a deadly rebellion against God, seeking glory for myself which could never meet my needs. What I really needed was the profound and powerful grace of Jesus Christ to reclaim my heart.

"When I was a young architect, Richard, I used to take a lot of photographs, and right up to about '79, when my faith really kicked in differently, I used to take photographs of buildings; naturally so, I was an architect. But when I took photos, I used to wait for everyone to get out of the way. I didn't want people to spoil the shot.

"When God began to fill that God-shaped hole in me, I stopped taking photos of buildings and I became interested in people. That may not sound like much, but it was one of the many ways that my focus changed. I changed. It was the same me, but I was gradually becoming quite different. I was aware that God's Spirit working in me was not only filling that God-shaped hole, satisfying the hunger and the loneliness, but He was slowly transforming my whole character. God was performing some kind of surgery on my heart the day that I took that plane ride. He was beginning to replace an identity that had become contaminated with the wrong kind of esteem, all the things we try to fill our lives with when we don't have the relationship with our heavenly Father that we are made for. My tears were an expression of the pain of that surgery, not because of the withdrawal of grace but because of the undeserved and lavish extravagance of it.

"I think if I had continued on my first track, if I hadn't met Heidi, and all that followed, I have no doubt whatsoever that I would have been a workaholic, probably divorced, maybe more than once, and a burnt-out wreck. Jesus talked about Himself as the bread of life that came down from heaven and he talks about the giving of living water. The Old Testament picture of that bread was the manna that came down to feed the Israelites. It was not something that you could stock up on to satisfy for the rest of the week, it needed to be gathered fresh each day. We need bread for our stomachs like we need air to breathe, or rice if you happen to live in the East. But Jesus wasn't talking about the physical when He said He was the bread of life. He was saying you can't live without feeding on Him, our daily bread, our ongoing communion. Give us this day our daily bread. That's how we are designed, Richard. In Him, we live and breathe and have our being. Any attempt to fill the tank with something or someone else still leaves us empty.

"Despite my numerous weaknesses, and some continuing insecurities, the more I have got to accept that God really loves me, that I am completely forgiven, a welcomed prodigal for whom He delights to throw a party, the less I feel the fear and shame of my failings, and the less I need to put on the mask of being someone I'm not. None of us have well-formed characters, Richard. In fact, we are all deeply flawed, fearful and insecure, and probably often lonely. But, if we are honest, we all have to say that we need God's help. His job is to put right in us what is wrong, and ours is to know that we need fixing, and also to know that God doesn't hold back His love until we are fixed. Besides none of us will be finished work this side of heaven, and yet Jesus still can't wait to see us face to face in the place He has prepared for us."

Richard no doubt pondered for a few minutes while we walked the river path and enjoyed the afternoon sun on our backs.

"Bob, I'm thinking back while you're talking about this, and about Saul on the Damascus Road and I'm going to ask you, was that experience that happened to you, on the plane, was it not something that led you to commit even more to going along a certain road? Did you see that as some kind of spur to develop your faith? I mean, why else would it have happened?"

Richard was always engaged and thoughtful, and for a moment, I considered his question. I asked, "Do you remember what words came from heaven when Jesus was baptised by John?" Richard hesitated for a moment and said, "This is My beloved Son in whom I am well pleased."

"Yes", I said. "It was an affirmative experience and not a conversion experience like Saul's on the Damascus road. That voice of affirmation came from Jesus' Father in heaven. What had Jesus *done* up to that time? Nothing that we know of. He hadn't yet performed any miracles, called out His disciples, or spoken any words that are recorded, except a very brief encounter at the temple when He was a child. I am learning that Father God says the same things to us from the very moment we return to Him. He takes pleasure in us aside from anything we think we may do or have done for Him.

"I think that when God spoke those words to me on the plane, that He had 'made all of this' for me, and that He had revealed His mystery to me, He touched something that had been previously completely contrary in my psyche. I didn't know how to receive unconditional love, only the affirmation that followed achievement. I'm still very much a work in progress now, but at that time I couldn't receive God's words very well. As the years march on, I think I am able to believe what was said more and more. 'You are also my beloved son.'

"God's love is gently transforming me. Like a good human relationship, memories, and trust build, and I think I am as much, possibly more impacted now by those words on the plane than I was at the time they were spoken. I am continuing to learn and experience that I can fully believe all that they convey. Perhaps, along with that belief comes the sense of joy. It's like the joy of a child always seeing his father's eyes light up and with his smile directed towards him. I don't feel I have to keep on apologising. I have come to realise that God truly loves me, though I still find it hard to grasp that He loves me in the same way that He loves Jesus. I know that also sounds pompous and preposterous, Richard, and yet it's nothing other than what Jesus says to His disciples in John's gospel, in chapters 15 and 17.

Chapter 14.

Hiroko

After Heidi and Norway, and my experience of encountering God in Malmo, my life was anything but smooth going. When I arrived that autumn to enrol at Rensselaer Polytechnic in Troy, upstate New York, the first people I met socially were Gary and Diane Roosa, who were converting a large house just off the bottom edge of the campus. They were Christians, in fact, the only Christians that I met that whole year, and without hesitation, they invited me to live in the house they had bought. It was on Ninth Street, Troy, across the Hudson River from Albany, the state capital of New York.

Downtown Troy and First to Seventh Street had completely disappeared. The buildings had been razed and there was nothing but grass down to the river. Every week. someone was torching a house for insurance and the fire service would make the pretence of extinguishing, but in reality, they just let them burn. I watched a nearby fire once and the crew just played their hoses right over the house to the next street knowing that if they put it out, they would only be called back when someone torched it again.

Ninth Street was poor black, and the streets progressed in affluence and became whiter in racial colour as they rose through the blocks which sloped uphill towards the higher end of the Rensselaer campus. I guess Gary and Diane were hoping to buck the trend by buying on Ninth Street. They could certainly buy cheap.

There was a small gateway entrance to the campus at the end of our street and, perhaps because I was one of the very few white faces around there, the Alsatian dog in the last house, who thought it his business to guard that entrance, would slink up to me every morning that I went into college. He would clamp his jaws around my ankle without properly biting, fix his eyes up at me, lift his lip and growl. After a few moments of impasse, he must have thought he had made his point and let me go on my way.

That dog and I developed an understanding, and I wasn't ever bitten properly. It wasn't a comfortable experience each morning, since I had been attacked and bitten by a dog when I was a child and roaming the country lanes alone in Kent. For many years, I had been extremely nervous around dogs, and I guess this was a kind of therapy, though, for the most part, I still remembered to pray.

The guy next door on Ninth Street was shot at his own wedding, and one time I had a bullet whistle past me when I was walking across a parking lot. It pinged the lamppost next to me. I thought a kid was probably just messing about from one of the windows of nearby housing. I didn't run for cover but rather just stood still and looked in the direction of the shooter.

Another time, a drunk held a knife to my throat one evening. He was probably wondering what a white guy was doing out at night in a black neighbourhood, but my polite responses in an English accent talked his tension down, from paring his fingernails into my face to an eventual warm handshake and a smiley goodbye.

It was a dangerous environment, but I was conscious in those early months after meeting Jesus that the Lord was with me and that I didn't need to fear. It was the autumn term of 1974. McDonald's opened their first UK restaurant, Muhammad Ali regained his heavyweight title by knocking out George Forman in Zaire, and Ronald DeFeo Jnr. murdered his entire family in Amityville, Long Island. But this was well before the days of the internet, mobile phones, and social media. Thankfully, my parents had no idea of the kind of place I was living.

The PhD I was doing absorbed my time. Gary and Diane were Christians but not churchgoers and there was no other invitation to a church. I had never experienced church anyway, and prayers at Gary and Diane's home were confined to grace at mealtimes. Bit by bit, I stopped praying and thinking about God. I had not read much of the Bible and that didn't progress either. Though I could never have denied the experiences I had had in Norway, their memory and effect began to fade.

In Oslo, the Children of God had had something called the 'Poor Boy' club, which was a vibrant music and social venue which I went to a couple of times. Wherever I travelled afterwards, I looked for it, and my assumption had been that this was where people who knew God met, as church had never been part of my experience in any way. But I never found another Poor Boy club and I realise now that there may have been just one other, in London, certainly not in a backwater like Troy.

Slowly, through neglect and ignorance, I was drifting away from God. I was unknowingly dismissing the pilot of my ship; the rocks were getting closer, and I wasn't even aware of it.

In the summer vacation of '75, when I had finished my thesis but planned to travel around the States, I had a surprise visit from Hiroko. She was, for that time, an unusual Japanese girl. I had met her at a party in London a few months before going to Oslo and we had become lovers. It was then rare for a traditional Japanese girl to be studying in London and all the more so in the all-male engineering environment which she had chosen. When she pitched up in Troy, it was a bait to a hungry fish who didn't realise the danger of a lure. Hiroko had her eyes on marriage.

We refrained from rekindling a relationship while she took a room in our Ninth Street house for a few weeks. I guess I had something inwardly nagging that it wouldn't be right now that I had become a Christian but at that point the inner guide to my conscience didn't have strong foundations. Despite having said back on that Bergen Street, 'Lord, I'll do whatever you want me to,' I didn't really know what it was he wanted me to do, certainly not in terms of how to live my daily life. Either way, the 'daily bread' was no longer being asked for, or delivered, and I had long stopped trying to pick up a Bible.

And so, when I agreed with Hiroko to sightsee in the summer vacation and to hitchhike around the States together, it was on the first night in a motel that she invited me to share her bed. From then on, my course was set directly towards the rocks.

Not only was Hiroko a traditionally brought-up Japanese girl but she had also brought with her a full Kimono, complete with wide Obi sash tied in the Taiko box knot behind. She wore it while we thumbed for lifts, and without it I doubt we would have covered half the distance hitchhiking around the States that we did. Car and truck drivers slowed to take a look, and many stopped to ask who we were and what we were doing. It wasn't difficult to then persuade them to give us a lift.

Hiroko knew someone in San Francisco, and we borrowed their car to visit the Grand Canyon and Las Vegas. Driving out of Las Vegas late one night, I was too tired to drive, and we decided to park up in a desert lay-by. It was dark and just as Hiroko had just started to say, "Are you sure you're on the track?" I managed to reverse over the precipice of a deep railway cutting. The car caught on the chassis and teetered at 45 degrees like in a Keystone Cops movie. After the shock of tipping backwards and suddenly facing the stars, we managed to scramble out on one side in the dark and reach the top of the cliff. There were a few small homestead lights in the distance, though it was a dangerous thing to go knocking on doors in deserted places at night. We struck it lucky and eventually got the car pulled off with a tow truck. Amazingly, there was no visible damage.

We had a few other scrapes from time to time, narrowly avoiding broken legs when ignoring instructions not to pass behind a mule line at the Grand Canyon as they were blocking our walk on the narrow path down. But Hiroko was really furious with me about the car and things were getting a bit tense between us. The writing was already on the wall.

Chapter 15.

Thumbs Up from Jesus

I hadn't planned on writing this chapter, but I needed a break when I had got to the end of the last paragraph. A friend, James, had given me the use of his mother's small cottage in Dorset so that I could begin writing this book. The cottage is in a tiny village called East Chaldon, or Chaldon Herring; it has two names. I had noticed that there was a church service at 11 am in St. Christopher's Anglican Church in the next little village called Winfrith Newburgh, and I was debating whether to go or not.

If I were to go, I was expecting it to be a sleepy little church, probably even colder than the cottage, and with a small elderly congregation. There was a cold snap in November, and I was staying somewhere very pretty but it would definitely have been at its best in the summer. I nearly stayed in the cottage to continue writing on the Sunday morning, but on a whim, I decided to leave the chapter about Hiroko unfinished and to go along to church.

When I arrived, it was a lot warmer inside than I had expected. Several radiant heaters beamed down nicely on about 30 elderly heads and there were one or two friendly greetings on arrival, including that of the woman vicar, Jenny. She was robed, and probably the youngest amongst the elderly congregation. I say that, but then half were probably in their mid-sixties, as was I. I don't feel old, and maybe they didn't either.

I was handed the liturgy book. I'm not used to Anglican liturgy, but I had thought maybe I should go and see if God had anything to say to me that morning, but I wasn't at all expectant.

I took a pew seat, not at the back, and certainly not at the front. As I sat down and scanned the backs of heads, I noticed, two rows straight in front of me, what I took to be a Japanese woman. I could tell from her hair that she was at least Oriental, and she stood out amongst the genteel village folk who were all clearly very white Anglo Saxon. I couldn't see her face, but she seemed about my age.

The 'hymns' were actually choruses I knew, but they were from a book we used to sing from about thirty years before. When it came time for 'the peace', most of the congregation greeted most others, all mutually acquainted it seemed, until, in turn, it came time for the Japanese lady and me to greet one another. As she looked up at my face, her jaw dropped. Then she gasped, a full-on gasp of complete surprise, and then she returned to her seat. I was bemused by that, and it certainly grabbed my attention, since not long beforehand, I had begun to write about my travels with my Japanese girlfriend some 40 years before.

I settled back to listen to the sermon, which was all about Christ as King, but then vicar Jenny interrupted her biblical thread to say that she felt she should recount a story. What she recounted was a story of a Christian travelling back and forth across America, just as

I had been writing about as it related to me. By now I was thoroughly tuned in.

This travelling woman had noted the lamentable state of every restroom she had to use and complained about it frequently in silent prayer. 'Why, Lord, if I am a child of yours, do I have to put up with these wretched facilities, dirty toilets, soggy paper towels on the floor, hand basins and mirrors smeared with soap and grime?' She sent up her silent prayer- complaint every time she needed to stop somewhere for a comfort break. Then, one day, after a similar silent complaint was directed at heaven, Jesus spoke to her. "But I'm the next person coming in after you," He said.

Those words really brought her up short. She remembered the Lord's words: 'Truly I tell you, whatever you did for one of the least of these brothers and sisters of mine, you did for me.' She realised that instead of complaining about other people's filth, and the state they left the washrooms, she should clean them for Jesus, who was going to be the next person to come in after her. And so she did. From then on, and every time she used a restroom, she picked up the sodden paper towels from the floor, wiped the basin and mirror, and left it as best she could for the unseen guest who followed.

As vicar Jenny recounted this story from the pulpit, the Lord began to speak with me, not in an audible voice, but internally, and as I reflected. I began to feel a new kind of sorrow for those years I had spent drifting after first encountering the Lord in Oslo. I felt sorrow for contributing to the mess, such as the wounding I was to inflict on my girlfriend Hiroko, and many others, rather than doing what I could to help clean up their lives and prepare the way for Jesus to come to them.

The emotional pressure was really building as I was captivated listening to the story that Jenny had broken off to recount. Tears were beginning to show, and I tried to wipe them away without anyone in the church seeing.

It came time for communion, which was ministered at the front rail, and starting at the front, pew by pew, folk went out to file up the aisle for bread and wine. As the Japanese lady stood up, instead of going forward into the aisle, she turned around 180 degrees and looked straight at me as I sat two rows back. There was a gap, and no one was in the pew between us. She smiled the broadest of long smiles, and then she stuck her thumb up directly to me. There was no mistaking the gesture, it was direct and deliberate. This complete stranger turned around in a sleepy Anglican village church and put her thumb up directly to me, with a great grin on her face. To no one else, just to me.

Then God spoke, again not in words but to my spirit, and it was as if He was saying, 'I *was* with you all that time you were drifting, and 'messing up the washrooms' without caring for others. I have forgiven you a long time ago, and you are forgiven now.' And it seemed to me that the 'thumbs-up' was not so much from this woman representing my girlfriend Hiroko, because it wasn't Hiroko, but in all the coincidental circumstances of that day in the church, I knew that the thumbs-up was from Jesus.

I could scarcely make it back to the pew from communion. My eyes were so filled with tears and my shoulders were shaking. I really thought I was going to lose all control and have to run out. I managed to stay in my seat, but only just. I discovered nothing else about the Japanese lady. I looked for her after the service but didn't catch sight of her at all. She had left before we might speak and though I inquired, I discovered nothing more about her than that her name was Monica.

I have no idea why Monica had looked up at me and gasped, or why her thumbs-up and smile were directed to me. Perhaps she had a dream the night before, or a vision of my being there, or perhaps she was that way with every stranger, I won't know. But I'm writing this barely three hours from returning from that church and I'm still trying to be careful not to get the keyboard wet with tears.

Chapter 16.

Jesus Loses His Chihuahua

Hiroko and I moved on from the Western United States, reached Mexico and went on to see the sights of the Yucatan and the Maya ruins at Chichen Itza, not far from where Richard was to fish for tarpon. The excitement of sex was waning, and we had another big row. She decided to go to Acapulco and left me, which was OK, except that I had almost run out of money. I had been relying on borrowing funds from her for the remainder of the trip and it was more than 3000 miles back to New York. Hitchhiking in Mexico was out of the question, but I had just enough to buy a ticket for a slow train to the border.

The food vendors with their covered baskets of rice and beans, salsa and tortillas often seemed to be walking faster than the train as they peddled their wares to customers hanging out the windows. By the second night, the toilets had overflowed, and I woke up in my seat in the middle of the night to an inch of sewage over my shoes and soaking the rucksack which I had kept against my feet so I could be sure to keep it safe while I slept.

I think it had taken three days and three nights from Merida in the Yucatan, passing through Mexico City and Monterrey, and on to the border at Nuevo Laredo on the Mexican side, and then to Laredo across the Rio Grande into the U.S. By the time I had crossed the river border and found a place to begin hitchhiking to San Antonio, and then to head north through Texas, I was getting really sick.

There was almost no traffic, and the sun was ferocious. Not only was my stomach sick, possibly from a sewage bug on the train, but I was beginning to get sunstroke. I had called on a nearby house for water, but I only succeeded in acquiring a begrudged small cup of something stale and lukewarm. After most of the day in the sun and I was beginning to need some help, a young Mexican guy approached me, and he was crying.

His name was Jesus, a common Spanish name. He wiped his tears and said, "Someone has stolen my Chihuahua." He also told me that his uncle was a truck driver who could maybe give me a ride in the morning and that I could stay at his house that night. The thought of a lie-down and a cool drink was a good offer, and so I picked up my rucksack and we wove through a couple of streets to his parent's place. He told me to leave my bag and we set off together to see if his uncle was in.

I didn't feel like staying on my feet but there was no option. We crossed a few more streets into a shanty town and along the railroad which passed through shacks on either side of the track. Jesus took me to his uncle's small shack where three girls, his cousins, were sitting on the veranda, just a few feet from the railway. He chatted with them for a while in Spanish and explained to me that his uncle was asleep inside. One of these three girls was deaf, dumb, and blind.

The sun was beginning to set, and it was getting colder. I was wearing just a pair of shorts and a t-shirt and dark glasses from the heat of the day, but Jesus wanted to get himself a sweater or jacket and so he said he would run and get one and be back in a little while. He left, the girls went inside, and I was left waiting alone on the veranda.

I waited for quite a while until it was getting dark and still there was no sign of Jesus, or anyone from inside the shack. Because of the route that he had taken me, I had no idea where I was or how to find my way back to Jesus' parent's house. The shack door was just a split curtain hung across the entrance and I thought that maybe I should see if the girls could help, but there was no light on inside.

It was a very primitive shanty town, and I didn't think they even had electric light. I felt that I had no choice but to venture in through the door curtain very cautiously. Straight away, I sensed several bodies asleep on the floor in the dark. There was not enough light to tell properly, but there appeared to be no beds, just several sleeping bodies on a wooden floor.

I bent down and gently shook the first one awake and as the child sat up, I could just make out that it was the deaf, dumb, and blind girl. I'm sure she quickly sensed that I was the boy on the veranda, and as she got up, I could just see that she went to go behind a curtain that was hung across a back corner of the shack.

By that point, I was quite ill from the sun, dehydrated, and not really thinking straight. Putting myself in that family's home, a stranger, a gringo, in the dark at night in their shack, and wearing just shorts, a t-shirt and dark glasses, - amongst the daughters, - what was I expecting?

The uncle that Jesus had spoken of had never seen me, but when he was woken by his disabled daughter and came suddenly from behind the curtain, he didn't hesitate to throw a punch to my chin which knocked me straight through the door curtain and flat on my back on the veranda. He quickly followed me out, and picking up broken bricks, shouted, 'I keel you!'

I have no doubt that he did intend to kill me, and, in those circumstances, no one would have thought any more of it. My body would have been dumped somewhere and I might have been a missing person to this day. I managed to get up just as the bricks started flying and ran across the tracks, ducking and diving as the missiles followed.

I spent the whole night trying to get help. A couple of Mexican policemen smoking in a patrol car were completely disinterested, and so was anyone else I tried to talk to. By first light, I was about to find somewhere safe to crawl into and lie down when I eventually recognised where I was and found my way back to Jesus' house. He wasn't there but his mother was. She lamented that her son, 'Shouldn't be doing that sort of thing', but suggested that maybe my backpack was in the garden. She seemed to go straight to a small plastic bag with my passport in it, but that was all that was there.

I realised then that there was probably no stolen Chihuahua, that the uncle may or may not have been a truck driver and that the mother seemed to know exactly where to find the passport. Maybe that was so that the police and British Consul didn't need to be involved. I'd lost another night's sleep, I now had a sore chin, as well as heatstroke, and a sick stomach. Jesus had managed to get a rucksack full of my smelly and unwashed clothing.

I was still not able to eat anything, but needed to drink copiously, and came close to being seriously assaulted again by a large Texan, accompanied by his two young daughters. He saw me taking a pee around what I thought was the back of a restaurant, but it turned out to be next to a frequently used rear entrance that they appeared from.

It took about a week to get home to Troy. I had eventually got a ride from the Mexican border towards Austin, Texas, which was given to me by a hugely fat American returning to his wife after a long stint away working in the oil business. I was not eating at all due to my stomach problems and was obviously so stick-thin that it must have seemed as though I was desperately in need of fattening up by his standards and I'm sure that he had the best intentions to be hospitable at his home.

He took me to his house where he greeted his equally fat wife very passionately. They chatted, patted, and canoodled on the sofa in front of me as though I wasn't there. Then they really started to get carried away with each other. No doubt their passion was burning after his long absence, but I didn't want to stick around and see just how hot it was going to get so I left quietly. I don't think they even noticed me leaving.

The next ride was from an equally huge trucker. He took pity on me and, talking on CB radio, arranged ahead for other rides from truck-stop rendezvous where huge plates of waffles, pancakes and eggs were always consumed, dripping with maple syrup and butter. I mostly sat, silent and unnoticed, amongst those guys who talked stories of being on the road. The first conversation was about cab break-ins: 'A nigger broke into my cab last night, so I shot him. Right between the eyes.' I kept my head down. I kept quiet. I was happy not to be noticed.

I was passed from truck to truck at freeway stops, often being put in the truck sleeper compartment behind and above the driver seat so that I could lie down. Sleep was elusive. Lonesome long-distance truckers always wanted some conversation. I was thankful to finally make it back to Ninth Street.

When I reached Troy and walked along my street in tatty shorts, my t-shirt, and dark glasses, I was happy that at least I didn't have to pass by my old friend the Alsatian. But the other dogs in the street didn't recognise me. I was a white stranger in a black street and several of them attacked. They went for my clothing and took most of what remained of my shorts off my backside.

I arrived at Gary and Diane's front door to be greeted by them before collapsing. My stomach hadn't allowed me to eat for days, I was dog tired and soon went to bed in my own room. Within a short while of falling asleep, I was awoken by a racket outside my door, and I went out to remonstrate. It was a young lad that I hadn't seen before, someone in trouble who Gary and Diane had taken in while I had been travelling. I learned later that he was on the run from one of the many New York street gangs in the 70s.

He had never met me, and my curt reprimand for waking me with his clatter didn't go down well. He grabbed my windpipe and tried to throttle me. As we were writhing on the floor, Gary came upstairs and broke up the fight. I was taken to hospital the next day coughing blood. I don't think I really recovered my health from that week or two, not for many years anyway.

At that time, I wasn't praying. Not once did I even think to ask Jesus for help. I have since learned that prayer doesn't come naturally. We need the help of the Holy Spirit to be able to pray, and I was leading my life in a way that meant that the Spirit of God had become very subdued in me. My heart had been ruled by my own selfish desires instead of being ruled by Jesus. He was there watching over me, of that I have no doubt, but like a mist descending over a glorious view, He had become obscured, and then I had stopped looking in His direction until I no longer remembered His presence, or listened for His voice, or picked up the Bible to read His word.

Chapter 17.

Some Have Entertained Angels Unawares

Richard and I had covered quite a bit of the storytelling of our lives. We were enjoying getting to know each other and weaving here and there through our various histories and so we arranged to meet again for coffee quite soon. I somehow got into talking about my early experience of reading the Bible, soon after my shipwreck years when I had drifted through all sorts of catastrophes without Jesus being the pilot of my soul. We chatted and I was bemoaning the fact that people often think they know what the Bible says when they don't because they haven't read it.

"You know, Richard, the typical things are like Adam and Eve and the apple. An apple isn't mentioned, it just talks about the fruit of the tree of knowledge of good and evil. Several examples come up at Christmas such as the inevitable three wise men. Nowhere does it mention three of them. These magi would almost certainly have travelled in much larger groups in those days, it's just that there are three gifts, gold, frankincense, and myrrh, and we are so used to seeing three men depicted on Christmas cards because of that.

'Goodwill to all men' is another, sung in the Christmas carol, when what is written is that the angels announce glad tidings of great joy to 'men of goodwill,' or, as many translations give the sense; peace towards those on whom God's favour rests. That's not the same thing at all as 'goodwill to all men.'

"The only thing my mother would quote, perhaps yours did too, was, 'Cleanliness is next to godliness.' No doubt it lends authority to washing hands before dinner, or after going to the toilet, yet Jesus berated those who made a show of being clean on the outside but inside they were a 'grave full of worms'."

"I could quite easily practise my Christianity without the Old Testament," Richard said. "I think we can take the New Testament as the beginning of the story, can't we? There's too much of the Old Testament; it's establishing, what's the word, provenance? It's a concerted attempt to prove. I have no quarrel with that, but when you read the New Testament and what Jesus got up to and what He said and how He related to the disciples and the general population, now that's pretty convincing stuff."

"But presumably not to you, Richard," I contradicted. "It's not convincing to you." "Oh yes, that part of the Bible is," he reaffirmed, with some surprise at my comment.

"Let me explain," I continued. "Jesus Himself confirms the Old Testament scriptures. That was His Bible, and also that of His disciples, and the Jews at the time, because the rest of it hadn't been written. So, on the road to Emmaus, not long after the resurrection, Jesus joins two followers going to that village from Jerusalem, but they don't recognise Him. He explains to them, beginning with Old Testament Moses and then all the prophets, all the things concerning

Himself which were written in those scriptures hundreds of years before His coming. There was a lot of stuff for Him to cover but we are told it was a seven-mile walk between Jerusalem and Emmaus, so that's maybe a couple of hours, probably long enough to explain quite a lot. The point is, Richard, that Jesus affirmed that the Old Testament provenance, as you call it, was all pointing to what we read about Jesus in the New Testament. The whole Bible is about Him.

"I love the Old Testament. Not all of it. Some of the genealogies written to establish exactly what you are calling the Jewish provenance and history can be a bit tedious unless you dig deep. But there is so much that is pointing forward to Christ, just as He explained to those two on the Emmaus Road.

"Take Abraham, for instance, the father of the Jewish faith. Sarah was 90 years old when she gave birth to the long-awaited and promised son Isaac, and Abraham was 100. There is amazement, laughter, and great joy in the birth. But then, much later, when Isaac was probably a young man, God tells Abraham to take his beloved son, his only son with Sarah, - God says he has to take him on a three-day journey, and to sacrifice him. Abraham and Isaac reach Mount Moriah where they had been told to go, and which is probably where Jerusalem was later founded.

"When they reach their destination, Isaac asks, "We have wood for the fire, but where is the lamb for sacrifice?" Abraham replies, "God will provide for Himself the lamb for the burnt offering." And sure enough, just as Abraham is about to bring his knife down on his son, who is tied to the makeshift altar, God calls out from heaven. "Stop! Now I know that you really do love and trust God because you haven't withheld even your only beloved son." Abraham looks aside and there is a ram with its head caught in thorns. The ram was God's own provision for the sacrifice.

"Christians see in this a clear picture of Christ's sacrifice to come. Indeed, by his complete trust in God, that somehow God would raise his son from the dead, Abraham is the very example of faith that New Testament scripture speaks of as our own salvation. The Abraham story mirrors God's provision of Jesus as our sacrifice provided by God, almost certainly at the same place where Jesus hung on a cross a thousand or so years later. I'm sure Jesus would have explained all this about Himself to those two disciples on the way to Emmaus."

Richard reflected quietly for a few moments before I continued. "In my journey of faith, I said that I had drifted somewhat, and I didn't take delight in reading the Bible again until about four years after returning from the States. I had my own small flat in Kentish Town by then and was working as an architect in Camden. I had still never attended a church and had no one to teach or encourage me but there was a longing for what was missing, even if I couldn't rationalise it or recognise quite what it was.

"On a tube journey home from work one day, I overheard a girl speaking to another passenger opposite her and it caught my attention. She reminded me of Heidi speaking to me about Jesus in Norway, and when this girl had finished talking to the passenger, she handed him a leaflet. I went over and asked if I could have one as well, which she gave me, and then it was time to get off. I stuck it in my pocket and forgot about it until that Friday evening when I found it again and saw that there was an evening meeting advertised in Earl's Court. I just had time to get there, and I decided to go.

"When I arrived, I think it was St. Philips or St. Jude's, I can't remember which, but what I do remember was an extremely pretty girl going up the steps as I was arriving. She said hello and I went in and sat next to her. I don't remember anything about the sermon except that there came a point at the end when the preacher said that there was someone there who had drifted away from God and that this was their time to come back. I was transfixed, and at that point I shot up out of my seat with such speed and compulsion that I think the preacher was quite startled. I was hoiked to my feet in a manner that completely surprised me too. I didn't shout out, 'That's me!', but everyone could see that it was.

"And so, God began his rescue from my drifting, and I began a new leg of the journey with Him. But getting back to the Bible, Richard, it was not long after that I was in my little first floor flat in Kentish Town when there was a ring on my bell from the communal front door downstairs. I went down one flight to answer and when I opened the door, there was a very smartly dressed man and a woman who I didn't know. They asked if they could come in, and for some reason, I just said 'yes' without inquiring why, or who they were. They then followed me up one flight to my flat.

"At that time, I had converted my tiny one-bedroom place into an open plan room. I had knocked down every wall that I could and as my then future wife still remembers, there was not even a door to the bathroom, and the kitchen was no more than a cupboard opening to the main part of the sitting area. It looked nice, and suited a bachelor who rarely had guests, though Enid was not so keen when she moved in after we married.

"The strangers sat down at my dining table, upright and very formal. I remember their silhouettes as they sat with their backs to the street windows. I offered some tea. 'No, thank you.' I offered a jam sandwich, which was about the height of my culinary skills at that time. 'No, thank you.'

"Then the man said, 'We have come to bring you this', and he produced a large brand-new black study Bible. It was only then that I thought to ask, 'Well, who are you? What are you doing here? Where have you come from?' But there was no direct answer; not even polite conversation, or any clues about them at all. They gave me the Bible, not a cheap one I later realised, but a study Bible with notes, and maps, and all kinds of lexical information and commentary. They sat there for a few minutes, declined all my attempts at hospitality, and then got up, politely said goodbye, and left.

"Richard, from the moment I opened that Bible, I was completely absorbed. God spoke over and over again as I read it and for two years it was like I was being accelerated through a crash study course, making up time for those years of drifting. It carried on like that until I think God might have thought it was time to live some of it out rather than grow a fat mind.

"From that time on, I began to understand that the Bible is a spiritual book. Unless the author Himself speaks to you through it, it will seem a dry and dusty thing, or at best an academic pursuit. It's not a bad thing to study it that way, but it will disappoint, and probably be put back on the shelf to get dusty. It's really only transformative when the Spirit of God begins to speak through it, and we become nourished by its daily bread.

"The majority of households have one or two copies, but they sit on a shelf or in a drawer. Without that vital connection to the Author, so many try to pick it up but struggle with it. The Author has to be at home in our hearts before He can turn the light on to what's written in those amazing pages. Otherwise, it's just like trying to read in the dark. When the Spirit of God turns the light on to the pages that He has authored, then even the Old Testament comes alive. Next time you read it, Richard, start by asking God to speak to you through it. Ask Him to turn His light on for you." "I will, Bob. Any suggestions where to start?" "Start with a gospel, Richard, maybe Matthew or Luke, for a chapter or two at a time, and then perhaps try the first few chapters of Genesis. There are lots of good Bible reading plans. Let me know how you get on."

Chapter 18.

Liver Cancer

When we met again, Richard had just seen a doctor. I knew he had some health issues and I asked him if he was OK, and he asked about my son Jack who was recovering from some quite difficult maxillofacial operations at St. Thomas' Hospital. Richard said he needed a check on something but that he was fine, and the conversation turned to our health. Richard said, "My childhood was severely affected by frequent bouts of very, very bad streptococcal tonsillitis and it held up my growth and development." "It looks as though you made up for it later," I interrupted. "Oh yes," he said, "I made up for it later all right! It would have been around about 1939, and I was having a particularly bad bout of tonsillitis when the GP, we had a very good GP in Chelmsford, when the GP said he was going to prescribe a new miracle drug called M & B 693. It was sulphanilamide, pre-dating antibiotics, and it came in little tablets made by May and Baker with 693 stamped on them, reputedly the number of experiments taken to formulate it. It was the first of the sulphur drugs and did the trick for me and it was just in time for the Second World War too. You could use it for gonorrhoea, and it may even have changed the course of the war because, in 1943, it cured Churchill of bacterial pneumonia pretty rapidly. Reportedly he took it with whisky or brandy, reminding his nurse that man cannot live by M & B alone.

"Now, I told you, Bob, that I was a pathologist after the war, and I got into a business that was very, very early in those days, and they were beginning to measure responses to antibiotics. I was very friendly with a guy who had become a senior person at Beecham's when they were just beginning to develop the new oral penicillins. The result was that I left bedside medicine and was involved in research that produced some remarkable new molecules. I was offered a job in Brussels to be director of European clinical research and I was privileged to be part of a group that pioneered beta-blockers for hypertension, high blood pressure, which had never been used up until then. It was all pretty heady stuff and I guess what I'm saying to you is that my mind was miles away from Christianity for all this time.

"I was also involved with pioneering cancer drugs too, and l was pretty lucky to be fit and well throughout that time, but in December '02, when I was involved in distributing these little packs for testing the stool for occult blood, you know, you have to take a little bit of faeces on a stick and so on, someone had said how unpleasant it was. So, I took one home to see what it was all about, and I did it, and it came up positive. I thought, 'Yeah, this can't be right,' you know, get on with the stuff you have to do, so I didn't pay any attention.

"But I happened to tell my GP about it quite a bit later and he thought he'd better arrange for a colonoscopy, a light and camera with a tube to reach the colon, and they found I had early colon cancer. This was five days before my last grandson was born, and I thought 'well, at least I'll get to see him born'. It was taken out successfully by a brilliant surgeon, but I do look back on how foolish I was. I was a doctor, yet I lost five months by dithering and ignoring it.

"I had what might have been a final follow-up in 2007, with a CAT scan of my gut, when the radiologist said, 'You've got a secondary cancer in your liver'. Now, during the time I was a medic, the survival rate for my age for colon cancer, caught early, was about five years for about 60%. But if you got a secondary in the liver you couldn't do anything about it. That was it.

"By then, I was an FRCP, a Fellow at the Royal College of Physicians, and I was mixing with the cream of the profession, and during that time, three of the men that I respected most as clinicians failed to act on the evidence of their own colon cancers, got secondary liver cancer, and it finished them. All my teaching up to that time told me that a liver secondary is a sentence of death.

"I trotted over to my surgeon, and I suppose I was expecting tea and sympathy. 'Oh,' he said, 'yes, we'll have to take that out. I'm going to phone Professor Nariman Karanjia right now.' Nariman turned out to be a brilliant liver surgeon and my chap discussed me with him right there and then on the phone. He said to him, 'When can you do it?' Now I don't know if you know, Bob, but the liver is a very vascular structure with lots of blood vessels wrapped around a brown mass and you've only got to touch it and it bleeds copiously. But I found out that they had just developed a technique with a certain kind of instrument that dissolves all the liver cells and just leaves the arterial tree. If you can find the artery which goes to the secondary cancer, you can take it out, close it off, and bingo.

"I went to see Nariman, and he said he had a slot in three days. That was eight years ago now, and I had a letter from him last year saying that based on my history, he would rate me as cured. I'm now eight years on from the liver and thirteen from my colon cancer, something that would have been unthinkable at one time. I'm very lucky."

Chapter 19.

Pray for Bob, He's in Trouble

The fact of Richard's remission lasting well beyond what he could have expected was clearly something he didn't take for granted. Many times, in later conversation, he mentioned that he felt he was on borrowed time. I guess that his medical insights brought all that into even sharper focus, with the knowledge that most people in his situation would not have survived.

"I've been meaning to ask you, Bob, have you seen anything like what they call, 'healings'? Supernatural stuff, you know what I mean. As a doctor, I'm not sure what I think about all that."

"Yes, I have, Richard. Like you, I had a childhood problem. I had stomach pain from my early years, and I know that my mother took me to the doctor while we lived in Kent, but it was neglected. Someone mentioned 'acidosis.' I don't know if that was a general term in the 50s for childhood stomach pain, but nothing was explored or done about mine. 'He'll grow out of it,' was, I think, the main prognosis.

"My pain carried on for years and was worse seasonally and with certain foods. I was getting blood in my stools in my mid-20s, and it was getting particularly bad around the time I encountered my first church in Earl's Court, the one where I told you I jumped up out of my seat. I was 27 years old.

"Not long after I joined that church, it moved from Earl's Court, and we began to meet at Putney swimming pool. There were a series of three evening healing meetings there and when they were announced in the diary, for some reason I felt sure that I was going to be healed if I went along. I did go to the first one, and that night the pain was worse than ever. I went again the second night and the same thing, worse still, and again the third night.

"The day after the third meeting, I needed to see a doctor and he sent me to the Royal Free Hospital for x-rays. They gave me that wretched barium meal to drink, then the x-ray machine broke down, and by the time it was fixed I had to drink a pint of the stuff again. I must have had a silent tear running down my cheek as I sat in my gown on the bed and the radiologist looked at me and said, 'You've had enough, haven't you?' My head was slumped on my chest, and I just nodded. I really had come to the end.

"When he sent me out to the corridor after the x-ray had finally been taken, everything started to go black, and I reached to the wall on my left and managed to connect with one of those emergency panic buttons. I could hear footsteps running towards me from behind and I was aware of being caught just before hitting the floor as I fainted backwards. It was lights-out until I woke up and was being prepped for surgery.

"They had thought it must be acute appendicitis, but It was something that hospital called acute ileal diverticulitis. I never saw any hospital papers and doctors later said it must have been Meckel's

Diverticulitis, which is a congenital disease to do with the umbilical cord, more likely to affect children. If there are going to be symptoms, it's usually from around the age of two years old, as was the case with me. Only a low percentage, mostly men, are born with this malformation of the small intestine. You must know all about it, Richard, so forgive me, but about two percent of those who have it have any problems with it. Mine was probably quite severe, and perforated, so I woke up after fainting having had part of my stomach cut out, which then shut down, and I spent at least a week on a catheter, nasal tubes, drips and so on, and retching black bile with a tube coming out of my stomach oozing from the wound. It was rotten.

"I didn't let my parents know. I had only just taken on a mortgage, and I had left paid employment to set out on my own. I don't think anyone connected with me knew where I was for a week or so. When I had recovered enough, and my bowels had started to work again, I could shuffle about the ward from time to time and I became aware of an intermittent background noise. It sounded quite unearthly, like a trapped animal howling somewhere in the woods.

I asked a nurse what it was, and she said, 'Oh, that's Julie; she's had a stroke.' When I had tracked down the noise, I discovered it was coming from a private room in another part of the ward. There was a television left on inside and there was some partially obscured glazing into the room, but I couldn't see someone in there. I decided to venture in. I shouldn't have done but I was curious about the unearthly noise I had been hearing. When I quietly entered, there in bed lay a beautiful young woman, very petite under the sheet as far as I could see, or possibly just very thin.

"I discovered later that Julie was totally paralysed by her stroke, but conscious. She was left in the bed all day with her head turned towards the television and a few times every hour, day and night, everyone could hear this moaning coming from the room, muffled by the enclosure but still loud enough to hear. When I entered, her eyes turned towards me and I asked that if she could understand me, she should blink.

"Just a few months before, and particularly during my earlier days of recovery, I had become very God-conscious again. I very much wanted to bring comfort to her but standing in front of the bed I had absolutely no idea what to do or what to say. I couldn't imagine what it must be like to be trapped, conscious, inside a body that doesn't work anymore and left, hour after hour, day after day, in front of the TV. And she was still so young, maybe near my age.

"Julie did blink to indicate that she had heard and understood, and so, I just said, 'Jesus knows about you, Julie. He does understand. He cares, he really does.' And then after a few moments, I didn't know what else to say and I left.

"Later that day, I was back in my hospital bed, and I overheard the nurses talking. They were saying, 'What's happened to Julie? She's stopped making that noise.' And so she had. For the remaining week or so that I was there, no one heard Julie's anguished groans again.

"Now, Richard, I have no idea what happened to Julie. She wasn't, as far as I was aware, healed physically. But who knows whether she hadn't been inwardly screaming out to God? Something like, 'Do you know about this?! Do you even care?!!' None of us knows what happened to Julie but I'm going to ask Jesus what that was all about in heaven, and I expect He will tell me. I also think I will probably be able to ask Julie.

"Getting back to your question about healing, Richard, I suppose this was all a prelude to what happened next for me. I recovered, was discharged, and didn't get any call back from the hospital or any check-up to see how I was doing, but everything was OK for a while. Then a few weeks later, one evening after supper, I remember I used to like those boil-in-the-bag fish meals, cod in butter was my favourite, real easy bachelor stuff. Anyway, sometime after supper, I suddenly got an acute abdominal pain. It wasn't just trapped wind or indigestion; it felt as though something had split apart. I started to shake, my teeth were chattering, and I thought my body was going into shock.

"It was in the days when you could call a night duty GP and I managed to place a call and unlatch the front door to my flat in case I was going to collapse. I did collapse, right across the inside of the door, but I was conscious when the doctor arrived, and I remember he had to push the door to move my body out of the way in order to get in.

"He got me up and onto my bed. I was still shivering, and my teeth were chattering like a wooden rattle at a football match. I could see from his eyes that he looked worried, and he called for an ambulance straight away. We waited together for about another five minutes but then the pain suddenly stopped, and I felt perfectly well. Quite suddenly, I felt a hundred percent, as though nothing at all had been wrong. The doctor just phoned to cancel the ambulance and left, and I went to bed and slept.

"The following morning, I was thinking about all this, and thinking right back to those healing meetings when I was so sure I would be healed by God, when there was a ring on my doorbell. It was Patrick. Patrick was the fiancé of the really pretty girl who had met me on the church steps in Earl's Court. Patrick had been one of my very few visitors when I was in hospital, and since his cycle route to college in Finchley could detour to pass my flat, he had called by on the off chance of saying hello. I invited him in for a coffee, we sat down, and I told him about what had happened the previous evening.

"Patrick was a gentle and hesitant soul, one of the musicians in the church, and after hearing my story, he suggested with some timidity that, perhaps, if I didn't mind, we should pray. He leaned slightly across the table and put his right hand on my left shoulder and prayed. I don't remember the words at all, but it wasn't a long prayer. It was something quite simple, like: 'Lord, please heal Bob of whatever the stomach problem is.'

"As Patrick began to pray, I felt a terrific heat in my stomach and then it was like a little ball of fire that ran backwards and forwards zigzagging from top to bottom through my intestines. Now, I know we have got yards of these tubes stuffed below our stomachs, but if you spent your whole life trying to sense the shape of them you wouldn't succeed. But I felt the zigzag shape running down, and from side to side, as this little ball of heat moved through them. Patrick felt something too, and he exclaimed, 'That's it!' And I exclaimed the same. We both knew that God had done something, and we talked excitedly for a while until Patrick thought he had better make a move for college. He checked his wristwatch and it had stopped at the time he had prayed and I had received my healing. Without realising, nearly two hours had passed since he came, and he said he was now probably too late for college.

"I have since seen quite a few healings, Richard. My wife's two are quite extraordinary and I expect I'll tell you about them sometime. I don't know why God didn't heal me sooner, why I wasn't healed when I went for prayer at those healing meetings, why, when I did go, things actually got worse, or why I had to have surgery. Perhaps it was so that I could bring some comfort to Julie, though I know God didn't put me through that just so I could meet her. Yet, even if He had, I wouldn't now have it any other way. I don't begrudge all that time, or the years of pain, not at all. I just know that God was jealous over my healing and although the surgeons were involved, He very much wanted me to know: 'I am the God who heals you'."

I had spoken publicly of this healing a few times while I was in the same church as Patrick, but I lost touch with him around 1994, when the church had some difficulties and many people moved on. It was another twenty-three years before we met again with the opportunity to chat; at the 90th birthday party of the mother of a mutual friend who had also journeyed with us in those early church years.

I asked Patrick if he remembered our encounter of that day in my flat, and we began to reminisce. "Yes, of course," he said. And then he began to explain something about that day that I had had no clue about. He had been on the other side of London when he thought God had spoken to him saying something like, 'Go and pray for Bob, he's in trouble.' He had felt compelled to make the detour and come, but nonetheless was very uncertain and hesitant about praying for me. He told me that it was quite a battle within him to come, and as far as he was concerned, it was a huge act of faith to try and overcome those inner voices that were saying that he shouldn't; that God might not have said anything at all. But he did come, and he prayed for me, and I was healed.

Chapter 20.

She Died in October

By now, Richard and I had had several rendezvous over a few months, and I thought that we had a genuine friendship growing. He kept asking me whether the kind of thing he was telling me was going to be useful for the book and I kept reassuring him that it didn't really matter whether it was or not, that I just enjoyed his company. He also told me that there were some things that he had never spoken to anyone about, and also that he thought he would start reading the Bible again. I was praying for him and hoping that he might begin to open up more to God. I hoped that there would still be plenty of time. Richard told me, "When I was a house doctor at Tooting, I got very caught up with an attractive woman from Ireland. We got quite serious for a while; she was a Catholic. Talking with her and being with her, I wondered if I ought to convert. I acted on that and went and had about half a course of instruction at Farm Street. It's a very up-market place in Mayfair, off Park Lane, where I had several sessions. I realised that to become a Catholic, I would need a leap of faith that I was incapable of, and I couldn't do it. "Instead, I met and married Mary. She was a sister at St. George's when I was a houseman, and you know, that was the cliché, doctor marries nurse; we all did it, and life went on. After about thirty years, we were not getting on. A lot of that was my fault because I was moving from job to job and she wanted a settled life, which is fair enough. I suppose it was selfish of me, but I was doing all the things I wanted to do, you know the story; my career was becoming really quite exciting, for me, anyway, but Mary and I divorced in 1992. "Quite by chance, I came across a nurse who I had dated when I was a houseman in Chertsey in 1956. She was married and living in Canada by then and I had known them on and off. Her husband had a condition called familial hyperlipidaemia, which means that his blood cholesterols were genetically way, way up, and the life history of familial hyperlipidaemia is that they usually get massive infarcts in their mid-forties." "What?" I asked. "infarcts?" Richard explained, "It means 'stuffed'. The arteries get stuffed, and he had a massive coronary thrombosis which he just about survived but it left him with the equivalent of very severe Alzheimer's. That was when I bumped into her, and it just happened. We got together. I couldn't marry her because she was still married to Tom but we both looked after him. Not many people know this, by the way. I don't talk about it much. Blanca was from Spain originally, Pamplona, where the bulls run, and she was a lapsed Catholic and we talked about this at some length, and for various reasons then, I sort of went back to church off and on. She came with me and that was fine; then Tom died in 2000.

"We had a great time together, a really great time. I was with her for fifteen years and they were happy years of my life. We spent part of the time in Richmond, and she spent part of the time in Toronto where she had some business to look after, and she knew the place well. Then Blanca phoned me one day from Toronto, in July '06, and she said, 'Richard, I had the funniest experience today on the Metro'. She had fallen a couple of times and couldn't remember where she was, and she couldn't remember where to get off. She had lost her way.

"Well, she had been living there for twenty-five years; she knew it like the back of her hand. I met her at Heathrow on July 13th and took her home to Richmond. She looked haggard and weak and moved like a little old lady. Obviously, something was going on. I was deeply shocked. I was going to Parkside clinic at the time because of my colon cancer so I took her with me and said to the radiologist, 'Look, there's something going on here; I haven't got a GP for this, but would you accept me referring her to see what's going on?'

They did a brain scan, and she had a very rapidly growing malignant cerebral tumour. That was mid-July, and our happy life together was effectively over. She had operations, went into a nursing home when I couldn't manage any more, and by mid-September, I am not sure she knew who I was when I visited. I felt completely devastated. She died in October.

"I spent my days walking around Richmond feeling pretty ghastly. She meant a hell of a lot to me. That's when I passed the front door of St Mary's, and matins were about to start. A very, very nice lady was by the door asking if I was interested in coming in. I said that I was brought up in a village church. Before I knew it, I was in the door."

Chapter 21.

Barbara and Other Affairs

I told Richard about the various loves of my life, mostly short and pretty chaotic affairs. I had several in those drifting years before I walked up the church steps in Earl's Court.

One was an older woman, about forty, but I don't think she ever said her age. I met Barbara in Rome when I was there for a year with a Rome scholarship. She lived in Paris with a younger lover who was studying law and she had a little boy by him, but she was spending some weeks alone at the American Academy in Trastevere, on the other side of Rome to the Accademia Britannica where I was living.

Doing a postgraduate year in Rome was fantastic but lonely. There were not many scholars at the British School and nearly all were painters or sculptors. I was the only fine artist who was studying architecture and so when we were invited to show our work at the Uffizi in Florence, I was naturally delighted to be included, but the others weren't pleased for me at all. For some reason, they took the very superior stance that an architect had no right to show alongside a painter or sculptor and so they sent me to Coventry.

We had a long dining table at which everyone sat for meals, in the courtyard in the summer, but otherwise, in the large dining hall. There were no more than a dozen students in the school, plus occasional guests, but whenever I went to join the table at mealtime, someone said, 'That seat is taken,' even if it wasn't. There was no place for me to sit, and day by day, I either had to be by myself in another part of the dining room, which was intolerable, or retire to my own room. I mostly did the latter, and often got drunk.

It was then that I met Barbara, at a party at the school, and we soon started a relationship lasting a couple of years. She commissioned me to design a ski house for her in Stowe, Vermont, which I did. When I had finished in Rome and returned to London, I used to take some weekends to fly to Paris, and then to Normandy, where she also had a holiday home, a large oak-framed Norman farmhouse.

On the last occasion we met, she was going to meet me at the farmhouse, but I was instructed to first go to a local bar in Paris and to pick up the key to an overnight apartment she had the use of. She gave me the instructions, but when it came to asking the bartender about the key, he just shrugged. He clearly knew nothing about these arrangements. I sat down with a drink wondering what to do when a young man approached. It was her Parisian lover and father of her little boy.

It was a shock, but unbelievably, Barbara had entrusted her partner to deliver the key to that bar so that I, her lover, could pick it up. Not unsurprisingly, he had decided to confront me. He did so in a very polite manner and begged me not to go on to Normandy. But still, I insisted that I would. My moral compass gave very poor direction at that time when I was drifting from faith, and so he handed me the key and left.

Barbara brought her little boy with her to the farmhouse. The morning after my arrival she had to drive somewhere to do some business and left me in charge of him before she was due to return and take her son to a modelling shoot. The little lad was about four. He was on his tricycle in the garden, and, within two minutes of her leaving, he came scooting in through the back door. There was a very low threshold, the floor was almost level with the ground outside, but there was just enough of a lip to trip the front wheel. He went head over the handlebars landing smack on his chin on the flagstones inside.

There was a really deep gash under his chin which immediately began to pour blood, I mean, really pour blood, like his throat had been cut. I applied pressure and managed to hold the bleeding, but I had no idea where the first aid kit was. There was no phone, and I didn't know where Barbara had gone. I spent about an hour holding the gash together underneath the screaming boy's chin. It probably looked as though I had this little fella in a bloody chokehold, blood all over my hands and down his front, when Barbara finally arrived and let herself in. That was pretty much the end of our relationship. She was absolutely furious, not least because she had to cancel the modelling photoshoot for him. The trip had been a disaster, but I can now see God's hand in frustrating our relationship. Like so much else during those years of drifting from one relationship to another, starting with Hiroko and ending with Barbara, things were so often a complicated and painful disaster.

It was not long after we ended our fraught liaisons that I was handed the leaflet on the tube, went to the church in Earl's Court, and began to reconnect with God. Very soon after that, I had received an unexpected phone call from a stranger. She said she was a friend of Barbara's and, 'Would I like to show her around London?'

Her voice was dripping honey and I know that even a few weeks before her call I would have jumped at the chance of an interesting encounter. However, at that moment, and having just responded to the invitation to return to Jesus, I had an instant recognition of what it was all about, and a profound sense of danger. I simply said, 'No!' and put down the phone. I didn't utter more than that one word and I can imagine how rude I seemed, and her sense of unexpected rejection on the other end of the line, but I'm glad I did it.

I have thought about it since, and normally the thrill of an invitation or a chase would have been irresistible. I realise now that my numerous and usually short-lived relationships were not really about the relationship, physical intimacy, yes, but not emotional intimacy. I could put on an act. I could be humorous and charming and, in my own eyes at least, intelligent, and interesting. But it was skin deep, a persona that kicked in when it looked like there might be an adventure.

If I had reacted to that phone call as I normally would have, I think the entire course of my life might have changed. I couldn't have rationalised it at the time, but I think now that Jesus was no longer content with being just my Saviour. I'm sure that He was never content with just that, but He was now intent on being the Lord that I had invited Him to be when I had said: 'I will do whatever you want me to'.

Chapter 22.

I'm Lonely

I was getting quite stuck into the church I had encountered. There were about 150 young people at our services at the Dryburgh Hall, which was a hired space adjoining Putney swimming pool. It was a very dynamic time and along with many others, I had soon been given some responsibilities.

We used to have a service on Sunday mornings and then in the afternoon go up to preach on soapboxes at Speaker's Corner at the top end of Hyde Park. We would come back again, inviting whoever we could to come with us, and often conduct baptisms. Sunday was a very full day.

On one of those afternoons, I had thought I would give open-air preaching a go myself and had marked out the 'Roman Road', a kind of précis of the message of salvation from about half a dozen verses put together from the book of Romans. When I mounted the box to speak and to try to draw a crowd, no one was in the slightest bit interested and the people were all gathered around other speakers some distance away.

I don't have a loud voice; in fact, I have a pretty feeble one, but rather than step down from the box and feel even more stupid, I thought I would just read the passages that I had marked out from the Roman Road. Halfway through, a solitary gentleman who looked Middle Eastern, came and stood right next to the box, right up close in front of me so that he had to tilt his head up quite a bit to look at me. When I had finished reading, he just said, 'Read it again!' I was taken aback but I did read it again, from the beginning, and after I had finished a second time, he just looked at me and said, 'Yes! I believe it!'

It was then that I looked beyond him, quite some distance, to a crowd of people milling about, the ones who had been listening to someone else. About 50 yards away to one side I noticed a young woman by herself who was looking straight at us. As I looked at her, her face began to shine brightly. It really stood out as a glowing orb as I stared at her amazed. The man was still under the box looking at me when this was happening, but he then left, walked back towards the crowd and then towards this woman. They left together arm in arm.

God then showed me that this young woman had brought her father to Speaker's Corner to hear the gospel. These were conscious thoughts that came with a degree of certainty, and I really believed that was the case. After five years of drifting, God was beginning to speak to me again and there was a clear sense that He was taking charge of my life, and of my surrender for that purpose in a way that I hadn't done before.

Back at church that evening after this encounter, I was needing a wee after the evening service and went to the toilet. Louis, one of the young single guys there, came in at the same time. It had been a really exhilarating day, but I was feeling very tired, exhausted in fact, and for some reason, despite the day's excitement, I was feeling quite deflated when I went to use the gents.

There is a science about how men use urinals. It was one of the first lessons I learned in ergonomics at Nottingham School of Architecture. It is quite precisely predictable where a man will stand given any variation of existing occupancy. If it's completely empty, then a corner urinal is favourite to stop the possibility of others coming on both sides. Unlike ladies, men don't generally chat in public toilets, so when Louis came in, who I was barely acquainted with, he took up the predicted urinal with maximum space between us and offered the obligatory, 'Hi, how are you?' while facing the wall. I have no doubt that he was not expecting any significant answer or much more than a grunt.

Neither he, nor I for that matter, expected what came out of my mouth: 'Actually, Louis,' I said, 'I'm lonely.' Louis must have thought, 'Whoa! Where did that come from?' The last place to say something like that is standing at a gent's urinal. Louis didn't continue the conversation. But God heard me too, and He did.

Within a few days of encountering Louis in the toilets at Putney swimming pool, I had an invitation to supper. Enid and Lydia, two girls in the church, were cooking supper for my friend David and myself. I have since learned that we were not the only ones to be entertained in turns and that a number of young men experiencing their hospitality over the weeks. The girls were best friends. Lydia was desperate to get married, and Enid was determined to remain single, and so Enid was participating entirely for her friend's sake in the hope that Lydia might meet someone.

I had got to know a porter at the Royal Free Hospital and had cadged some flowers that were left at bedsides in order to bring an offering to the meal. None of us had any money those days but Enid now remembers the gift as being, 'from someone who had died.' I still remonstrate that I don't think they were necessarily from someone who had died, just left at a bedside.

I remember the evening for the smell of burnt poppadoms which greeted David and me as we arrived. David was a good-looking young guy and it felt as though I was there just to make up the numbers. I was definitely not in pole position that evening and I don't think I managed more than half a dozen words of conversation. Dates with Christian girls were new to me, and pleasant though it was, and having returned to my Kentish Town flat at the end of the evening dinner date, I expected nothing more would follow. I went to bed and slept.

At some point in the night, I suddenly woke up and sat bolt upright. There, just to the right side and near the end of my bed, was Enid. That is to say, it looked exactly like Enid, or rather Enid's top half, her head and torso, her bottom half didn't seem to feature. But my doors had been locked, and it wasn't Enid, it was a vision of her. It wasn't a dream, I knew that, and positioned there just for a second or two towards the end of the bed she looked at me and said, 'I love you!' and then she was gone.

I must have gone back to sleep fairly quickly, but on waking the next day, I knew without any shadow of a doubt that I was going to marry her. I already had a trip arranged to see my parents a few days later and I told them, "I have met the girl I am going to marry." I then had to try and explain why I didn't even know her full name, and why I knew practically nothing about her at all.

I had just about enough sense to know that I couldn't breeze up to Enid at church and say, 'God has shown me you're the one', or something similar which would be guaranteed to make a girl run. I waited and waited, and all the while my stomach was getting tied up in tighter and tighter knots, until one day after the service, I saw that she was serving drinks at the church coffee bar. I decided to pluck up the courage and ask her for a date.

In my earlier life, I had been used to at least trying a bit of charm and coming up with what I thought would be a killer chat-up line, but now it just didn't occur to me, and so I simply asked, 'Would you like to come out with me?' Enid looked at me and I could see her face drain. She went white and silent for so long that I was about to say, 'That's a 'no' then?' when she opened her mouth to say, 'Yes.' We agreed on a date at London Zoo. We have different recollections of how it happened, but Vera, an 80-year-old mutual church acquaintance, was asked to come as a chaperone. I strongly suspect that this must have been Enid's idea, though she insists it was mine.

Thus, Enid and I embarked on dating in April 1980. Neither she nor I had a bean between us. Dinner dates were often at the Wong Kei, then in Rupert Court before it moved to Wardour Street. It was fabled as the rudest restaurant in London and waiters would greet you by shouting, 'Go upstairs!', and by the time you had been similarly instructed at each floor, you would reach the top to be greeted with, 'Who send you up here? Go downstairs!' You could never guarantee eating in peace since you would be moved, midmeal, around a table, or even to another table, in order to fit even more people in. Heaven help you if you asked for a knife and fork: 'Why you ask for knife and fork?! You have chopstick like everyone else!' But it was good Chinese food, the rudeness was a form of entertainment, and Enid and I were getting to know each other within our very meagre budget.

It was at a slightly more romantic date, in the restaurant at the Indian YMCA on Fitzroy Square, that Enid first told me some of her past. She had been terribly ill as a child, first having an ear infection that had caused the loss of her inner ear. Then she caught tuberculosis of the spine, possibly from a swimming lake, which was followed by years in a sanatorium, and when she had just about recovered, she contracted polio in hospital.

Enid spent years in hospital, and also experienced a sense of abandonment when she had been moved, without her parents knowing, to another hospital some distance from her home. Her family was poor and managed only weekly visits on Sundays.

She had been in a full plaster cast for two years to straighten her limbs when, one night, after this body plaster had been cut off to allow for adolescent growth, and before being given a new one, she felt herself being pushed out of bed to the floor. Enid at that time had been almost paralysed, unable to walk, and should not have been able to get back into bed by herself. But she describes her fear of a certain red-haired nurse with hairy facial warts. Not wishing to be found by her on the floor in the morning, she somehow managed to haul herself back, albeit with the bed in considerable disarray.

When she had fallen out, she also sensed a peculiar thing, an aroma. A presence like nothing she had ever experienced before. In the morning, she was cross-examined by the warty nurse about the sheets being in such a mess and some things that were still on the floor, and she told how she had fallen out and got back in, something which the nurses thought should not be possible. That event led to a medical rethink and the resumption of physiotherapy, which they had given up on, and within a few years, Enid went on to run for her county.

It was while Enid was telling me this at our YMCA dinner date that I felt something strange happen. The only way I can describe it is as though our souls had been knit together. I had known in my head that I would marry Enid as soon as I had seen that vision of her, but now, a couple of months on, it felt as though God had performed a transaction in my soul. I fell in love then, though she had not, at that time, fallen in love with me.

Around the time that I had confessed my loneliness to Louis, Enid had vowed to the Lord that she would be happy to remain single and to serve Jesus as a single woman for the rest of her life, if that was to be what he had planned for her. From her side, our dating was reluctant and did not go that smoothly. On one occasion, we were setting off together for lunch after church and got on a bus to cross Putney Bridge towards Earl's Court where she lived. Without a word, she suddenly jumped off the bus without me and started to walk over the bridge. I got off behind her, but she was halfway up King's Road before I caught up and persuaded her to stop and talk. I think she just panicked.

It was three months into our courtship before we had our first kiss, on a roundabout in Brighton with the London to Brighton bike ride circling around us. We nearly caused a crash. By that evening, though I didn't yet know it, Enid knew that she had fallen in love with me too.

I think it was about midnight on that day when I was back in my Kentish Town flat, and Enid had returned to her rented room in Harrow, when she phoned me in tears and said that she was calling it all off, ending the relationship. I was stunned. "We had a good day, didn't we?" There was a tearful response saying, "Yes." "We're getting on well, aren't we?" And another tearful, "Yes."

Still on the phone, I then decided to tell her of the vision I had had of her at the end of my bed, and how I knew that she was the one for me. When I had done so, she proceeded to tell me of a dream that she had had, the night before I had first asked her out at the coffee bar when she had turned white, but still agreed to the zoo date. Enid told me that she had dreamt everything that had then come to pass on that Sunday morning as she served coffee, including someone who had playfully put custard in her hair.

Her dream had then shown me coming to the coffee bar and asking her out. But that is where the dream had taken a different course. She had then dreamt that I had been chosen to tell her that she was going to be thrown out of church. She had been thrown out of her home when she was a teenager and she had been asked to leave her first church, and so this was no doubt something that played on the difficulty of those previous experiences. It explained the white face and look of panic which I had seen, and perhaps the chaperone, but when we continued chatting on the phone late that night, we then both knew that God was at work.

We got married just three months later at a little church called the Orange Street Congregational Church, just below Leicester

Square and a stone's throw from the Wong Kei. The black and white wedding photos were done by an award-winning photographer against hoardings enclosing disused land which became the new National Gallery wing to the north side of Trafalgar Square. The hoardings had a fig tree growing against them and, with the use of Vaseline on the lens, the photos looked like we were in Hawaii. We did the whole thing with church friends for £50, including the reception in the crypt, the photos, my suit, and Enid's antique Victorian wedding dress. My parents and family came, and Enid's siblings, but her parents were not there. Her mother had died young, and she hadn't seen her father for years.

When Enid was about seventeen and she had finally recovered from those years of childhood illness spent in hospital, she was walking across public fields near her home. She passed a man who simply called out to her, "Jesus loves you!" She had missed out on childhood socialising and was very shy then, and so she ignored him and walked straight home, but after settling, she began to muse on the events of that day. In hospital, she had for years only been able to read books and occupy herself with an inner world of thoughts and it had long been her habit to while away time by recollecting anything and everything that might have happened during that day. She came to the point when the man had said, "Jesus loves you!" and so she thought, 'Well, if you are there, Jesus, if you are real, show yourself to me now.' And at that moment, the room was filled with a presence, the same presence, and the same unique aroma that she had sensed as a young girl a few years before, when she had been pushed out of her hospital bed.

From that encounter, and after two years of searching and finally tracking down the man who had spoken to her, Enid became a Christian and found her first church. She began to tell the family of her changed life but at seventeen, her father threw her out of the home because of her new faith. Like me, she went on to have many adventures abroad, until ten years on from those events, God brought us both together in London.

Over the weeks, I told Dr Richard all of these things and he spoke of his life to me. Our conversation meandered here and there. We were interrupted by waitresses, and telephones, and loo breaks, and the occasional shower on our walks together, but each meeting, for an hour and a half or so, had very little silence. We both always looked forward to our next rendezvous. We had developed a very close companionship.

Chapter 23.

A Bit of a Fall

"In sixteen days' time, I shall be in a position to connect with my haven of sanity again," Richard told me. "How is that?" I asked. "The fishing season opens, and I shall be able to use my stick on Ashmere Lakes again. First of October."

"Yes, of course, Richard," I said. "I'd forgotten. Time has flown. Perhaps I can join you at some point."

I think Richard had enjoyed my stories, and our traveling back and forth through the Bible, sometimes explaining the big picture and sometimes the detail. He had told me that he was starting to read it again and that's more or less where we left it before fixing a get-together for the following week which I put in my diary.

The day of our next coffee morning came, but Richard didn't appear. He had occasionally had trouble operating his email and his mobile, but once a date had been fixed, Richard had always arrived on the dot, so I was a little concerned but assumed there was probably just a mix-up.

It was only a couple of days later when Richard dropped into the Community Centre looking agitated. I had not seen him like that before. He apologised profusely and said that he had had a rotten few days, culminating in managing to wipe his mobile of all contacts, and his diary. He didn't explain what else was wrong, but he certainly wasn't his usual jovial self, and he left promptly. I sent another diary date when I had managed to check my schedule, and then again, didn't hear from him. It was in the first week of October that there was a message on my answer machine from a woman, who I later discovered was his first wife, Mary. Her message said that Richard had fallen and badly broken his arm and he was sending his apologies.

I tried calling back but couldn't track him down or get a response to messages. I knew he was turning eighty-four that month and that broken bones can be really nasty at that age. I was praying for him and wondered if the direction of our little pilgrimage together might now be changing.

It was just before his October birthday when I suddenly remembered that I also had his home phone number. Richard picked up pretty promptly when I called: "Richard Rondel!" His voice sounded just as it always did when picking up the phone, as though he were picking up while sat behind a grand desk in his consultancy office. When he heard my voice, he exclaimed, "Bob! Lovely to hear from you. I don't know if you know but I've had a bit of a fall and broken my arm. Bloody nuisance, right before the fishing season. I'm out of action for the foreseeable, I'm afraid, and I don't know when I'll be out and about again."

"Well, can I come over to see you, Richard?" "Of course you can," he replied. "I'm not going anywhere, but I don't want to put you out. I know how busy you are."

Richard told me where he lived, in a gated complex near Richmond Park, and we made arrangements for the following day, the day before his birthday. I looked forward to seeing how he was and to catching up.

Chapter 24.

The Parallel Universe and Prayer

When I went to visit, he had already opened the door to his flat so that I could let myself in and he was sitting on the sofa in a square and tall-ceilinged living room and with a blanket next to him. He wore a very generous pair of boxer shorts, a shirt, and his slippers. His right arm was in a padded sling and the first thing that he said was, "Bob, I've messed up our project." He shuffled to the kitchen, and I helped him make tea and pour the milk, and I had brought with me some chocolate biscuits and a sticky malt fruit loaf which we portioned together onto plates.

"Can we pick up and continue?" asked Richard. "Is it still possible? We've missed a few appointments and you will be going away soon." I replied that I wasn't concerned about 'the project' at all, and that of course we would continue, but "I *am* worried about you, Richard."

"It's ridiculous, Bob. I broke this two years ago," he said, pointing to his left arm with his right fingers poking from his sling, "and it took about a year to get really rolling again. Everything was fine and I was starting my slow cooker programme for the winter, and I had just started learning calligraphy. I have a friend at church who is a master at it, and everything was going along *beautifully*," he said, with a strong emphasis on the word 'beautifully.' He continued, "I suppose hubris comes to mind, does it?" No doubt Richard was thinking of ancient Greek gods punishing those who got too comfortable in their presumptions.

"That's not the word that comes to my mind," I replied. "If I can be honest, this is the expression that came to my mind, and I do apologise if it's an expression that you might not be used to..." It was now my turn to be circumspect and go round the houses, so Richard broke in saying, "Bob, you can't upset me."

"OK, Richard, so I think your life is being contested. Do you know what I mean by that?" "Yes, I do," said Richard. "I've had the same thought. I wondered if God was telling me I'd lived long enough." "No," I said, emphatically but gently, "that's not the thought I had at all! The thought that I had..." "Stop!" Richard interjected and leaned forward, "You've got my attention; I am already enjoying your visit, you're right on key, keep going," and we laughed.

I had watched a YouTube video just a few days before. It was a 90-minute feature on the life of Arthur Blessitt, a man approaching 75 years, who 40 years earlier was called in a unique way to carry a large cross through every nation on earth. The Guinness Book of Records shows him as undergoing the world's longest walking pilgrimage, carrying that cross through every nation, major island group and territory in the entire world, covering more than 41,000 miles, through deserts and deep jungles, through war zones and extreme conflict. He had completed this mission in Zanzibar quite recently, the last nation on the alphabet for his pilgrimage of evangelism.

I began to tell Richard the story of how Arthur received the call in his nightclub church on Sunset Boulevard in Hollywood. In the late '60s he was ministering to Hell's Angels, prostitutes, addicts, and hippies, when Jesus spoke to him and told him to take the cross that was in that nightclub church off the wall, to put it on his shoulder, and to walk across America; to take it out of the building and to take it onto the streets. Arthur resolved to do this but, almost straight away, suffered pain in his head which led to a partially paralysing aneurism and the prospect of brain surgery, with complete rest. He lay on his hospital bed wondering why Jesus wasn't telling him what to do about this when he realised that the Lord had already told him what to do, which was to take the cross down and start carrying it. Arthur described in the video how he would rather die with the wind in his face than flat on his back in a hospital bed, and so he took his tubes out, got up, and began his journey.

I told Richard of how Jesus had been with Arthur through countless trials and dangers but how the Lord had always rescued him and had always been with him. But right there, at the beginning of Arthur's life and calling from God, that life, and all that was to come, had been contested. He could so easily have stayed in his hospital bed.

"You see, Richard, I think that when someone starts to draw near to God, or God begins to do something new and significant in a person's life, this is often contested. Scripture tells us that Satan wars against Christians. He's not particularly bothered if a person has no faith or sense of calling, but when someone strongly becomes God-conscious, Satan can often stir things up a bit. In some ways, I wouldn't be surprised if there is a bit of stirring going on in your life."

"Some time ago, Richard, we spoke about your ideas of a 'parallel universe.' The Bible agrees, though not in quite the same way. There *is* an unseen spiritual world that is opposed to God. Jesus was acutely aware of it and Paul describes it as 'spiritual forces of wickedness in the heavenly places.' The effects of it are seen every day in our newspapers and on TV, and for that matter in our own streets, or at work, and often in our own lives."

Richard interrupted, "Bob, if I may stop you there for a moment. You are quite right that we began this conversation today with the thought that my life might be being contested, and I said I had been thinking along the same lines, so are you saying I have a battle on my hands?"

"There is a battle over all our lives, Richard, and the Christian ought to understand this, but not be afraid of it. We can be thankful that it has already been won, even if it's still being played out. It's like a winning chess move that can take place well before the end of a game. Once the move has been made, that's it, checkmate is inevitable, even though the game may still have a long way to go. Jesus effectively declared checkmate on the cross when he cried, 'It is finished!' But the days between then and the final checkmate, the demonstration of that victory, that is still being played out. Jesus did say to His disciples that they would have trouble in this world, but he also said that they were to take heart because he had overcome the world. The cross was an emphatic victory over God's enemies, and the last enemy of death will also be overcome.

"I wouldn't presume to say more than that those who trust in Jesus have absolutely nothing to fear. If I reach the age of 84 like you, Richard, God still has a call on my life. We can all continue to pray, bless, and communicate God's love to others right up to the departure gate."

Richard looked thoughtful and took up the conversation. "I have in the last few years; that is, one thread of my prayer is that I'm surprised to still be here, having had two episodes of cancer. I have sort of said, in effect, 'Why am I still here? You must have a purpose for me.' I still don't know what it is, but this longer life is a wonderful gift, a blessing, but I've thought, I must do something with it, I must understand why it is that I'm here and what it is that I'm supposed to be doing. 'Help me to amend what I am, and direct who I shall be'. That's the Anglican prayer."

I smiled. "Do you remember my plane ride? There *is* a great deal for us to do, Richard, but I'm sure that the purpose of God is not firstly what we will do for Him, rather it is what He has done for us and will do *in* us. We are His workmanship, and He will direct what we shall be. There is a wonderful scripture in Ephesians 2: 10 which says that we are God's workmanship; and the Greek word used indicates a poem: 'We are God's poem, created in Christ Jesus in order to do the good works that He has prepared for us beforehand'.

"God does do remarkable things through us, Richard, but I think that His first and primary purpose is that we should know the extraordinary and supernatural work of God *in* us. He wants to restore us to know to love and how to worship Him, and most importantly to enjoy being with Him. That's our ultimate purpose and fulfilment. Jesus quite remarkably said that this great work of

God is simply that we should believe in Him. Out of that poem comes His purpose."

Richard continued looking thoughtful and the conversation paused while he offered more tea and I cut another slice of sticky fruit loaf.

"I have told you before," he said, "that all sorts of things in my life suggest that I am lucky. Good things happen. I have sometimes prayed and quite clearly the things that I have prayed for have come about, but I haven't trusted it. I was going through a particularly nice phase recently, making new friends; my life ran on 'an even tenor', I think that's the phrase, and this fall has upended it all; a bit of trouble in the world I suppose. The first few days were pretty difficult. Every time I moved, I had two bone ends scraping: quite awful. I'm not a young man and, you know, you lose strength. I prayed a lot in those first few days for courage, just courage.

"Unless I can stay in a positive frame of mind, things drag on a bit," Richard continued. "I prayed for courage, and I have given thanks because all my friends and family have come out of the woodwork, to a degree that humbles me. People say, 'It's your daughter, it's your son, and so they should,' but I know that isn't always the case in families.

"My daughter and son have been especially good to me after my fall, to such a degree that I weep. I have also had friends coming in; the lady upstairs here has made me really great food. I have to protect myself against vanity, but I didn't know how much people liked me, perhaps even loved me. I don't think of myself with that frame of mind."

"You are very lovable, Richard, and I'm sure all this help is also an expression of God's love for you." "I hope so," Richard said rather wistfully, and there were a few moments of uncharacteristic silence.

"I'm sure that is so, Richard. I have come to know," I continued, "the extravagance of God's love and grace. When Jesus came, He came to declare freedom and liberty to captives, and also a new time of God's favour. It was also announced by the angels at Christ's birth: 'Glory to God in the highest heaven, and on earth, peace to those on whom His favour rests.'[1] God's favour is also mentioned for instance in Proverbs: 'For he who finds me finds life and obtains favour from the LORD.'[2] I've come to realise that people who trust in Him can legitimately see themselves as God's favourites."

"Should I think in that way?" Richard spoke with some puzzlement. "I don't think so."

"Well, we usually don't think of it like that, do we, Richard? And I don't mean that we should think of ourselves as favourites in any boastful way, or in any way that assumes any credit to us at all. God's favour is offered to every one of His children, and He wants all mankind to be reconciled to Him, but not many are prepared to receive that; not many want to 'think that way,' as you put it.

"I am reminded that the apostle John wrote of himself as, 'The disciple that Jesus loved.' He wrote that of himself in the third person, anonymously, so to speak. He certainly wasn't trying to boast, but I think that John had truly come to realise that God's love for him, as it is for you and me, was intensely personal and affirming, in spite of knowing his faults. The realisation of that love allowed him great

---

[1] Luke 2:10
[2] Proverbs 8:35

confidence in his relationship with the Lord. I'm quite sure that all God's children are His favourites and metaphorically His eyes light up as He sees us come to Him, just as any loving father would for any of their dear children.

"I've been a Christian for forty years and it's only in the last few that I could begin to truly say of myself, like John, that I'm a disciple that Jesus loves. God is pleased with the poem that He is writing in me. But the point is that He's writing it, Richard, it's not my poem to take any credit from; it's *all* His work. But I can be thankful and rejoice in His workmanship, and, painful though it is sometimes, I completely trust that every intervention is for my good.

"I think that for many years, my overwhelming sense was of falling short. I am acutely aware, Richard, of what goes on inside my little mind and much of that leads to unhealthy bouts of self-condemnation. I've mentally acknowledged God's love but usually thought that it wasn't really *me* that God loved. After all, how could He, knowing what I know about myself? Rather, I have often thought that it was only Jesus in me that God loved, or Jesus covering over the nasty me so that God's eyes didn't really see the real me underneath. It's taken all these years to really know that God loves the real Bob, even with the same love that He loves Jesus. That's not my invention, Richard, it's what Jesus said."

"Really?!" interjected Richard.

"Yes, really," I continued. "Those aren't my words; they are recorded in John 15 vs 9, and again in John 17 vs 23, as being spoken by Jesus Himself. It's very hard to reconcile that God loves me with the same love that He loves His sinless begotten Son, Jesus Christ.

"The sin and rubbish of my life are no longer in the way of God's love, and self-condemnation it shouldn't be in the way of my experience of it. My condemnation was placed on Jesus on the cross, completely. When we have faith in God's saving grace towards us, that extraordinary and undeserved sacrifice, then Jesus is not ashamed to call us His brothers and sisters. We become members of God's family and God loves these redeemed sons and daughters in the same way as He loves *the* Son. We are given the status of adopted children and in terms of the Father's love, that status is no different to the divine and begotten Son.

"We really are God's favourites, Richard. Look at the Song of Solomon, a wonderful and passionate poem about the love between two betrothed lovers. Christians see it as a picture of the love between God and His people. Indeed, the church is known as the Bride of Christ, and Jesus as the bridegroom. We are to be presented to our bridegroom spotless and holy. The Lord sees His betrothed proceeding with faith up the aisle of life in the same way that when I turned around and saw Enid on my wedding day, my eyes lit up.

"We so often think of ourselves as approaching the altar with a tattered and stained dress, smeared lipstick and hair all over the place. Jesus turns around and sees us as the most beautiful thing imaginable: His beloved, His betrothed, His glorious bride, His inheritance, spotless, all sin and stain dealt with.

"I know that doesn't sit well with any of us, Richard. I think it's because we don't really trust that Jesus has indeed dealt with our problem of sin; but He has. As Corrie Ten Boom, the survivor of a Second World War concentration camp, wrote in one of her books, 'When I confessed my sins to the Father, Jesus Christ washed them in His blood. They are now cast into the deepest sea and a sign is put up that says, 'No Fishing Allowed!'"

Richard had been leaning forward listening intently to all this. "I'll tell you something about my faith, Bob. I think it's rather superficial, but on the theme that you have just laid out, as far as it's humanly possible, I never pray for myself, recent pain being an exception. I always pray for my family, those suffering around the world, or whatever it is. I sort of say, 'Dear God, I didn't pray for myself so shouldn't I be getting a few Brownie points?' It's childish, isn't it? But that's what I do. I guess you are telling me that it's a misunderstanding of God's grace. I suppose, thinking about it, when you have an intimate and confidant personal relationship, for instance with your wife, you won't hesitate to say, 'My back aches; do give it a rub,' or, 'I'd love a nice cup of tea.' It's only with strangers that you might hesitate to be so free. I think I do see that."

"I remember telling you, Richard, that my father had to dress up in a stiff collar and to call his father 'sir.' I don't know if he ever knew him as 'Daddy', though in later years, with us children, he did refer to him as 'Pop.' When the disciples asked Jesus to teach them to pray, He gave them the Lord's prayer. You know: 'Our Father in heaven.' The word used for Father is Abba. We don't seem to have a direct English equivalent; it's an Aramaic word used by both younger and older children, and you hear it today as children call to their father. It is neither childish nor formal. It is used with intimacy and informality by a young child, and also with the status and respect afforded an older son. Perhaps it is more like the salutation of a Prince to his father the King, with an understanding that the King is his beloved father, but his father is also the crowned King.

"I meet many people who feel they can't bother God, except praying for the starving children in Africa, or wherever. I think, sadly, that this is diminishing both the bigness of God and the intimacy with which He wants to be involved in our lives. There is a passage by Paul in Philippians 4 which says something like: 'Don't worry about anything; instead, pray about *everything*; tell God what you need, and don't forget to thank Him for His answers. If you do this, you will know God's peace, which is more wonderful than the mind understands. His peace will keep your thoughts and your hearts at rest as you trust in Jesus.'[3]

"If I can just take us back a few moments," I continued, "you said that breaking your arm had humbled you because you realised how much family and friends loved you. I think it's the same with God. It's realising God's kindness and love for us that is the thing that most transforms us; realising that we *are* deeply loved changes us on the inside. It's not that *I* love someone, it's that someone loves *me*, and that realisation in turn helps me to love others.

"If we are hesitant about God's love, that we should only call Him Lord Almighty rather than 'Abba' for instance, or if we feel it's OK to pray about others but that we shouldn't bother Him about ourselves, then I think we are holding God's love at arm's length. That's why so many of Paul's New Testament prayers for the churches are along the lines that they would have the power to grasp how wide and long and high and deep is the love of Christ, and to *know* that love.

That, in turn, allows us to be filled and overflowing with God.[4] "If I can encourage you in anything today, it is to welcome Jesus into

---

[3] Philippians 4:6-7
[4] Ephesians 3:18

being at home in your heart through your faith and trust in Him, and to ask Him to help you grasp just how much He loves you. It's not something you can fully appreciate intellectually. God Himself needs to show you. But you can ask Him. Don't be English about it, Richard. When Jesus comes knocking, don't open the door a crack and say 'What are you selling? And whatever it is, not today thank you.' Invite Him in and let your faith make Him at home in your heart. Help Him to put His slippers on and make Him a nice cup of tea."

"I like that picture," said Richard, "and I've taken that all in. I will try to re-orientate myself, open up my home a bit," he said, pointing to his heart. "Speaking of a cup of tea, what about another…?"

Chapter 25.

Do You Know What Happens When You Die?

That first visit to Richard's flat was drawing to a close, but since we had spoken a little about him being conscious that he was living longer than he expected, I thought I might just ask a question after the kettle was boiled and another brew made.

"Richard, do you know what will happen to you when you die? Do you have any sense of hope and security about that?"

"No, I don't," was his reply. "I have a couple of friends who have workshops where they are advising me to go and talk about these things, but I'm just not into that. I suppose that I believe, 'what will happen will happen,' but that's not quite dealing with your point, is it?"

"Richard, if you believe that there is a judgment, if you believe that we shall either be with God or not, if you believe that there is a hell, as Jesus often spoke about, and if you believe that there is a qualification and disqualification from heaven to do with faith, then surely there can be no greater question to settle in our hearts. We might want to put a few more quid in our life insurance but that is nothing in relation to our eternal destiny. And so, God is very keen to reassure us about our eternal security. The apostle John says that he writes what he does so that we should *know* that we have eternal life. Not that we might have an uncertain hope or a reasonable expectation, but that we should *know*.

"Salvation, once granted, is not something that needs to be added to, or can be taken away. It was offered to all mankind through the cross: 'God so loved the world that He gave His only begotten son that whoever believes in Him shall not perish but have everlasting life.' It is offered freely to all. Our part is to receive it through repentance and faith.

"We spoke about God working His poem in our lives, Richard, but the verses in Ephesians just before that speak of salvation being by grace, through faith; it's nothing we can do for ourselves except to receive it by trusting that it is what Jesus has done for us.[1]

That way, no one can boast that they contributed any kind of qualification for heaven. No one ever has, and no one ever will.

"Sadly, I come across a lot of teaching, and this is a feature of many denominations and other faiths too, that implies that salvation is by our works, whether we have lived a good enough life or not, or sometimes that salvation by faith is not quite enough, that we need to add something else to our faith which sufficiently tops up the credit. It implies that we must add our little bit of good works, or that we must not eat certain foods, or dress in certain ways, or not fail to pray at certain times or attend worship on certain days; the supposed

---

[1] Ephesians 2:8-9

qualifications are endless. But salvation is only offered by grace, Richard..."

"But," Richard completed the sentence, "we must receive it by faith." "Yes, that's it," I concluded. That's exactly it."

"Well, Bob, you have given me a lot to think about. I think that this is perhaps one of the more significant conversations that we have had. I think, and perhaps this might tell you whether I have understood or not, but I think that I will have to rethink some of my attitudes towards my faith, and also my conversations with God."

Chapter 26.

Jam and Prayer

I have mentioned that Richard often went round the houses. Soon after breaking his arm, one of his excursions began after a considerable silence between us. "Bob, I was wondering. This isn't something I'm used to, and I'm not sure it's right. I suppose, what I'm saying is, but I'm rather uncertain about it ...."

"Richard!" I gently interrupted. "I saw a programme last night. It was about someone who was teaching English manners to wealthy foreigners, mostly Russians. They were sitting at a table in a swanky London hotel enjoying a very posh tea and cakes, and the tutor explained to his pupil that if he wanted the jam, he certainly wouldn't reach across to take it. He wouldn't even ask, 'May I have the jam?' What he should say to his companion is, 'Would you like the jam?' His equally well-bred companion should then say, 'No, thank you, would you?' Thus, in a very roundabout way, he would get the jam without actually asking." I paused for a moment and then asked, "Richard, would you like me to pray for you?"

"Yes! That's it exactly!" and we both laughed.

"Richard, Jesus said that we often don't have because we don't ask." I got up from my chair and went over to gently lay my hand on his right shoulder and beginning with 'dear Abba Father', I prayed for Richard and gave thanks for him. I prayed that God's Spirit would grant this dear man the power to see the Father's love for him, that he would be blessed, that he would be able to see God's face shining upon him, and that his arm would be healed. "Thank you," he said when I had finished. "I have never had that before."

Chapter 27.

What Happens When We Die?

When I went to visit Richard a week later, the door of his communal entrance was again already opened for me, but I had phoned ahead to say I would just be a minute in coming, and he was in his hallway waiting for me to arrive. He seemed excited.

"Come in, Bob. I want to show you something on my laptop." As he led me towards his study Richard explained, "You laid a healing hand on me last time that you came and prayed for me. I broke this arm on the 26th of September, about a month ago. I had an x-ray on Wednesday and the orthopod said that I was fast beginning to lay down bone, and the physio also said that it was *incredibly* early. These professionals were quite impressed. If you look in my study, I've got the x-ray up on the screen."

Richard opened the study door and showed me the x-ray of his upper right arm which he had placed on the screen ready for my visit. To me, it looked horrendous. The broken bone was clearly visible, like a green stick that was split with the top part sticking outwards and with a sharp point protruding into muscle. Richard saw my expression and pointed to the screen. "No, look, Bob, you see that?

That's already new bone bridging the gap. That's what both my surgeons think is *remarkably* early healing. Come in and talk to me while we make a cup of tea."

Richard's emphatic excitement was very evident, and he invited me to feel the lump in his arm, which was very obvious once I put my hand there over his shirt. We managed the tea between us in the kitchen and he asked if he could tempt me to a chocolate biscuit. When we had sat down, he began to explain his injury.

"It's a spiral fracture. If you take the humerus bone, in isolation, around the centre of the shaft is a spiral groove and that's where the nerve lies and so if you fracture it, the break tends to follow that groove, a sort of weakened point. I have wondered whether they can plate it and I've taken two opinions, but both say that it's too near the nerve to risk anything. I could end up with a floppy arm, useless. The main thing at my age is whether you have got osteoporosis, but I'm told my bone density is quite good."

"The main thing is whether you can cast a fly again," I countered. "Ah, yeah, well, I'm not counting on that, but I'm doing well, and I rather think your prayer might have a lot to do with it. How are things with you?"

It was the day before I flew to Ibiza with Enid and two friends, Chris, and Pip. Chris had just finished a management role for the rugby world cup and very much needed a break, and so did I, and we had decided to visit for a week with my daughter and her boyfriend who lived on the island. Two days after returning, I was due to retreat to the writing cottage in Dorset and knew that I wouldn't see Richard for a few weeks.

"Where are we on our journey, Bob?" asked Richard. "We have been meandering happily quite a bit, haven't we?" I said, "but just because I'm going away soon doesn't mean that we are near the end of the road. I am expecting to continue this when I come back, or even if I manage a break in between."

"Good," Richard said. "I had hoped so. I think last time we spoke I mentioned that I was really quite surprised to still be alive. Death comes to us all, of course, but I've been thinking about what actually happens to us when we die."

Richard continued with his thoughts; "It's hard to separate sentiment from what might be reality. Sentiment says that in some way you make a connection with your antecedents. I was watching a programme last night about Tibet and the Buddhists and their religion, and whatever they do in this life will weigh in the scales for reincarnation and if they do well now they go up a level and all life is sacred, and so on. You think about Hindus, or Muslims and what they think happens for them; 70 virgins and what seems to be a better version of worldly pleasure. We can't all be right, can we, Bob?

"At heart, we seem to create a structure which helps us to believe that it isn't over. Don't ask me what *it* is. But I have this fancy of transit, transit from this state to another state. I said before that in my hospital work, occasionally, you are with someone as they die and I can't believe that what was, until that moment, a soul, with thoughts and beliefs and ethos and love, I can't believe that..." Richard clicked his fingers, "that it just stops. What do you think?"

"I've seen someone I knew die in front of me, Richard, and I've watched the colour change drain through his body. The last words he spoke were to me. 'Can I have ten copies, please?' It was when I owned a high street copy shop. Who amongst us would imagine that our last words might be, 'Can I have ten copies, please?', but this fellow, Mr Johnson was his name, he just dropped dead of a massive heart attack right in front of me. I have no sense of what happened to his soul. I didn't really know him, and I simply have no idea, other than I do know that God knows how to judge rightly."

I began to recount what had happened to Enid's mother Ivy. She had died when she was about 40 years old. Ivy was dying of cancer; she came out of a coma, looked at Enid, who was by her bedside, and said, 'It's all right, Enid, I'm going to be with Jesus.' And then she died.

I was also privileged to know what happened to her father Donald. We had not long been married when I woke up one morning and said to Enid that we urgently needed to go and see him. I just had a strong sense that God was urging us to do it quickly, and so we went straight off to Birmingham that day. Enid hadn't seen her father for years, but she believed he was in a hospice, also dying of cancer like her mother had. When we arrived and had found out at reception which ward he was in, Enid went in to find his bed.

Donald had become a very large man after the war, which had probably brutalised him since he had spent some of it in a prisoner of war camp, and Enid remembered him taking some of that brutality out on the children. He hadn't been able to come to our wedding, he and I had never met, so there was unresolved history with Enid and a sense of trepidation for both of us.

Enid thought it best to be the first to see him at his bedside, before introducing me, and so she went into the ward alone. After a few minutes, she came out saying she couldn't find him. We inquired again of the nurse and were both led to his bed together. From her memory, he had been perhaps twenty stone, but in front of us was a man of about seven stone. I had been prepared to meet someone who might be a bit difficult, according to Enid's experiences, but lying in the bed was someone who looked absolutely radiant, and smiling as soon as he saw us.

Enid introduced me as her new husband and there was just a little polite chat between the three of us when her father turned to Enid and said, 'Enid, I met Jesus last night.' Our jaws dropped to the floor as we looked at each other and searched for words. 'What happened?' we asked Donald. Then, he told us that one of Enid's Christian cousins had visited the previous evening, with her husband and their seven children. The children had all lined up at the foot of the bed and been beautifully behaved which prompted Donald to ask, 'How is it you are such good children?' Apparently, they all replied in their various ways that it was because of Jesus being with them.

Enid had been praying for her father for years, but Donald explained that after her cousin and family had left the hospital, it had prompted him to ask Jesus if He could be with him too. And thus, at my first and last meeting with Donald, there he was saying that he had 'met Jesus last night.' He was radiant, absolutely shining, and so far from the harsh father she had known. That was why Enid hadn't been able to recognise him when she had first come into the ward.

He wanted to know what he might be able to do for whatever days he had left, and we explained that he might simply pray and enjoy being with Jesus. I think it was the next day that he died.

When I had finished telling this to Richard, I said, "I am completely certain that Donald is still enjoying being with Jesus now.

The wonderful thing also is that without any words being necessary, all that conflict between Enid and her father was resolved. There was complete forgiveness and reconciliation, and the slate was wiped clean."

At varying times in our chats, I had also mentioned to Richard what happened to my parents. There had been no further conversation about faith with my father, not since my disastrous first attempts on returning from Norway. He went on to have at least three more heart attacks and triple bypass heart surgery. It had been a close thing each time, and, at one time, my mother was convinced she had lost him, but he hung on until he was eighty-five.

Each heart attack starved him of a little more brain oxygen, and for the last three or four years, he was losing his memory and doctors thought he was also developing aggressive dementia. He once hit my mother and knocked her to the ground but had no memory of it. It took a long time before he could accept from her, and from others, that this had actually happened. When he had accepted it, he was deeply sorry.

It was a slow deterioration for Dad, and towards the end he spent several months in a small back bedroom in their Cambridge home. It overlooked his large and beloved garden, but when I visited, he was often in bed and not eating a great deal. The bedroom windowsill was too high to see his garden except for the canopy of our huge old pear tree which had been part of an orchard before the houses were built.

Like Enid with her father, I had been praying for my dad for years. At every visit to Cambridge I was hoping for something; a conversation, a prayer together, just something that might recover the lost ground of the last thirty years or so since I had become a Christian.

It was on one such visit that I was determined to try to talk personally and not just cover the usual banter about work, children, and holidays. I asked him if he remembered all those years ago when I had attempted to tell him what had happened to me in Norway. Our conversation did open up and I mentioned the love of God that I had experienced over the years and much of my understanding of the gospel of Jesus.

I was no longer throwing scripture balls at the coconuts, but I managed instead to speak very gently about the love that I knew Jesus had for my dad, and I asked him if he would like to pray with me and invite Jesus into his heart.

He said that he would, and we prayed together, and after we had finished, and with tears streaming down his face, he said, 'It's taken all these years to come to this.'

Not long after that, Dad went into hospital and his memory declined sharply. At one point, when I was by his bedside, he suddenly looked at me with panic in his eyes and said, 'Where do I live? Is it Sparrow Castle?' At my very last visit, he was no longer able to lift anything to his mouth which had become very dry, and he asked me to clean his teeth for him. I did, and he dribbled the toothpaste down his chin and uttered an expletive. That was the last word I heard from him, and I was sorry it was that way. It wasn't long before he died, and I have no idea whether, at the end, my father could remember his bedroom prayer. But I know that Jesus did.

My mother was harder to talk to. It's not that she didn't talk, it's rather that she didn't stop talking, especially after Dad died. She had suffered from a hyperactive thyroid which was removed when she was younger, but my mother seemed always to be a bit of a taut string, talkative, anxious, and 'nervy', as she would sometimes say. We once timed her silence on a car trip from London to Brighton and it amounted to just two minutes. It was my marriage to Enid that had helped to redeem my relationship with my mother. Enid quickly became the daughter that Mum had never had, and she also became 'Mum' to Enid.

We moved Mum from Cambridge to Richmond soon after my dad's death and she settled in a warden-assisted flat right in the town centre, within a few minutes' walk of everything she needed, including us. Still, however, if the subject of 'religion' came up, she would dismiss it immediately with, 'Oh, you can do whatever you did to your father when I'm on my deathbed.' I think she had some notion of 'last rites', or a final confession. On more than one occasion, my mother insisted that she knew she was going to live until she was 85, like Dad, and then go.

She had, in fact, turned 83 when she was deteriorating a little. Not much, considering that for half her life she had been almost permanently on antibiotics with a gynaecological infection, but there was a slight heart irregularity and her GP wanted her to have an angiogram. She went into West Middlesex Hospital a couple of weeks before Christmas and then promptly had a fall getting out of bed to go to the toilet. She got MRSA where she had damaged her nose and by the time that was under control it was practically Christmas, but they had one last slot on Christmas Eve to do the angiogram at Hammersmith Hospital.

Enid and I were very much looking forward to having her back with us in time for Christmas Day, and we were going to be joined for lunch by an elderly widowed neighbour. It was about mid-morning on Christmas Eve when we received a call from the hospital. The call didn't say much but that we needed to get to Hammersmith Hospital straight away. When Enid and I arrived, we weren't told anything but were asked to wait in an unoccupied area of a ward near where we thought my mother was having her procedure. Eventually, someone came and told us that she was having a stroke, that she was in the midst of it right then, that we could see her but that they were going to rush her to a stroke unit in another hospital. One of us could accompany her in the ambulance.

We both briefly saw her on the trolley and when she saw us, we could see that she was gripped with fear by what was happening to her. She made some attempts to speak but only a strange moaning noise came out. I remembered Julie in the Royal Free Hospital some 34 years earlier.

Enid accompanied her in the ambulance, and I followed by car to A & E at Charing Cross Hospital where they have hyper-acute stroke facilities. We were positioned behind a screen and could see the crash team racing here and there trying to save her.

A doctor came out to us and said, "Your mother has had a serious stroke," and he explained some detail of what was happening. "If we are going to try to save her, we have a new drug that might dissolve the clot. Will you consent that we try it?" We had little idea what all this meant, and we consented, as I'm sure anyone would.

The drug may have kept my mother alive, but she remained completely paralysed and was left with just minimal facial movement.

It was clear over the following weeks that she was fully conscious and in extreme distress, and sometimes in great pain from muscle cramps. She was then moved to Kingston Hospital where Enid and I visited daily. Sometimes she would be asleep and sometimes we could talk to her, and she could communicate with blinks and slight nods. I think just once or twice she managed something like a word, but it wasn't possible to understand.

Doctors told us that she wouldn't last long. At an early stage, we were asked if we consented to feeding through a stomach tube and we did, not realising, or being informed, that should she linger on the hospital would be obliged to keep her alive. They could refrain from giving life-supporting intervention, but they couldn't withdraw it once it was given, even though there was a clear statement to that effect in her will. We were hugely conflicted over her suffering but also very grateful that any life and death decision-making for the family had been removed.

We expected her to die, but she continued to hold on. We were told that her infection, or pneumonia, would not take long, but it did not come. She lingered for one month, then two, and then three. All the while, it gave Enid and me, and one or two visiting friends from church, the chance to talk to her, and pray with her, read Bible stories, and tell her day by day how much we loved her and how much God loved her. She couldn't run out of the room, and she couldn't hold us at bay with her own endless chatter. Enid and I began to realise that despite her suffering, this was God's grace and mercy for my mother. For the first time in her life that I knew of she was only able to listen. Our prayer was that God would finally get her attention.

Mum fought to stay alive, and I think for the first two and half months she probably expected to recover and go back to her little flat. She had had a minor stroke a few years before and had recovered completely. One day, when she seemed particularly awake, we decided to tell her gently that this wasn't going to happen, she wasn't going to get home to her beloved flat in Richmond. We found her sufficiently responsive at that time such that we could ask if she wanted to pray with us, and she nodded her 'yes'. We spoke the words for her, acknowledging sorrow for keeping God out of her life, and finally she nodded her assent to asking Him to forgive her and to come and be with her. At each sentence, she nodded slightly and then closed her eyes at the end and as we said our goodbyes for that day.

The next day Enid and I noticed a change. We could see that she had been crying a lot. I had only ever seen my mother crying once when she had thought she had lost Dad. When we arrived and she saw us, she continued her tears and wept for a long time while we sat with her.

When Enid and I spoke about it later, we knew that she had finally given up and that she was now ready to die, three months after her stroke. And sure enough, we soon had a call to say that she had got pneumonia. We spent the last hours at her bedside. Her breathing was shallow, and she was no longer conscious. She had worn a hairpiece for most of her later life because her thyroid problems had resulted in considerable hair loss. Not being able to wear her wig in hospital meant that we had been seeing my mother's remaining natural hair which, by then, was pure white and just like the tufts of wool you find on a country fence. There were some scissors by the bedside and so I clipped a little from her head to take home.

For hours, I remember counting exactly eleven breaths, and then a great gap before her body heaved to breathe again, with exactly eleven more breaths to follow. And so that repeated, hour after hour through the night, until there was no final heave of her chest, no more strength in her body to take a breath, and she was gone.

I know that others might look at all this and blame God for my mother's suffering. But I am so grateful that, at the end, she found herself in a position where she was finally persuaded to bend her will and reach for God's love. I don't believe that this would have happened if she hadn't been so pinned down in extremity and suffering. Enid and I prefer to see those months as God's mercy for her in the last days of her life rather than His indifference to her suffering. It was in fact an answer to our prayers, though we could never have wished it that way.

When Richard and I were drawing near to the end of our conversations about this, I tried to directly address Richard's question about what happens when we die.

"I suppose I'm telling you these stories, Richard, because, like you, I have seen people at or near death. You asked about what happens after we die, and I think our very brief encounter with Enid's father, Donald, is a good pointer. Jesus had so clearly come to be with him just before he died. It was what he had asked for, and the presence of God radiated from him with great joy when we saw him.

"I think there is another death which confirms what happened to Donald when he died. You may remember the thief on the cross. His life, like Donald's, had no doubt been rather brutal and brutalised. Shortly before dying, that thief had recognised who Jesus was. He recognised his own wrongdoing in life, and he had asked for Jesus' help. He turned to Jesus and said, 'Lord remember me when You come into your kingdom.' Jesus had simply replied, 'Truly, truly, today you will be with me in Paradise.'[1]

"I think the order of those words is significant. He didn't say you will be *in Paradise* with me, but rather, *'with me* in Paradise.' The point is Richard, that being with Jesus *is* our Paradise. We need nothing more than to be with Him and He with us. That was our Lord's promise in John 14, that He would take us to be with Him where He is. If we are united with Him in this life, we will also be with Him in the next.

"Richard, I could tell you all the stuff that the Bible talks about concerning death: the resurrection of all the dead, the judgment, the new heavenly bodies with which the souls of believers will be clothed. I could talk about all of this because there is a wealth of information in the bible concerning life after death. I suppose it is summed up when Paul says in I Corinthians chapter 2: 'No eye has seen, no ear has heard, and no human mind has conceived what God has prepared for those who love Him. But God has revealed it to us by His Spirit.'[2] There's a lot that could be discussed, but the most important thing to know, to be sure of, is whether you will be with Jesus."

---

[1] Luke 23:42
[2] I Cor. 2:9

Chapter 28.

You Are about to Die!

It was time to put the kettle on again and break out another chocolate biscuit. With these reflections on death, and Richard's advancing years, and because he nearly always brought up a comment about borrowed time whenever we met, I suppose I was always conscious that the end could come suddenly. I remembered something that had happened a while back during my early church years in London. When we settled again with our drinks, I began to tell him.

"Richard, you said you weren't sure of your eternal future. Today and every day is always the most important day to be sure of that because, unlike my mother, and she was wrong, none of us knows when we might die.

"Let me tell you something. Years ago, not very long after my drifting in faith and soon after I joined my first church, I had a few attempts at preaching at Speaker's Corner. One time it was from a soapbox, but mostly not. It was possibly my very first attempt at speaking without a box to stand on that I had no trouble drawing a crowd because a heckler had managed to do that for me. He was a very tall and good-looking guy with a public-school accent, smartly dressed, whereas, in those days, I think my fashion sense made me look a bit of a mess.

"This guy was a professional heckler and probably a frequent visitor to Speaker's Corner, and I was very much an amateur preacher. That is, it seemed that he liked to spend his weekends ripping apart Christian apologists who had their soapboxes there. This was before it became a favourite location for Muslim preachers. He had interrupted what I was saying and had gathered quite a large crowd which seemed to follow him, and which had completely encircled us both.

"This guy was up quite close in a one-to-one encounter with me, and he began by generally making fun of the way I looked. 'Why is it that all Christians look miserable like you, and wear John Lennon glasses and dirty-old-man raincoats?' He poked a lot of fun at me, and the crowd was loving it. He finished by asking me in a cocksure way: 'If, at my last breath in life, I repent and believe, will I go to heaven?' He obviously knew the theological answer, and probably the example of the thief on the cross that we just talked about, and so I was obliged to concede that, if he truly repented, then indeed he would go to heaven.

"Unknown to me, there was someone in the crowd who had been attending my new church. I didn't know him, but he was a young black guy who had been part of the crowd and was listening to all this from behind me where he stood at the front rank of what must have been about 100 people. When this last question had been posed by the heckler - would he go to heaven if he repented at the last - this black guy jumped forward between me and the heckler and pulled a switchblade from his back pocket. You could legally carry something like that in those days. He pulled it out and in one deft movement clicked open the knife and held the blade pressed against the heckler's throat. He looked him in the eyes for a moment and said, 'You are about to die. Repent!'

"The crowd gasped. Of course they did. All the sniggering and snide comments stopped and there was a complete hush. For a few moments of shock, no one knew whether this was for real or not. The drama of it was very real, and very powerful. The crowd must have taken a little while to process what was going on, as did I, and to realise that there was no intent behind the threat. But there was a message. The point had been made, and the heckler slunk off with his tail between his legs.

"Just like my mother, none of us know when we might die. We certainly can't reserve the option of last-minute repentance, or last rights as my mother had put it, all the while living a life as we please now. God is gracious though, and I have no doubt that there are many who reconcile at the point of death. God's promise that everyone who calls on the name of the Lord will be saved is as true then as it is when we are young, but none of us can rely on deciding, at the last, that we will put ourselves right with God. Salvation and repentance do not belong to us; they are gifts from God. Today is the day to be sure that we have asked Jesus for this gift, to be sure that He is with us and that we will be with Him."

"I'm going to stop you there," said Richard. "I love your stories but, just backtracking a bit, and taking into account all the stuff in the Bible that you mentioned that talks about life after death; I gave you some of my thoughts, you know, a parallel universe and so on. You didn't react to any of them. Is that because you were listening to what you didn't really think yourself, but you wanted to revert me to that which is the truth, if you see what I mean? In other words, were you listening but thinking, 'You're on the wrong track, brother?"

Richard was sharp in his observations. He must have noticed all my reactions, or lack of them. Perhaps he was too polite to press any comment at the time. "Yes!" I said, and we laughed.

"So, you don't go along with what I think in any way?" asked Richard.

"Richard, I do want to know what you think. But I also know what I think. And I think by now that this is a dialogue between friends who can respect and trust each other. However, I can say that I have come to trust that the Bible is the word of God. There are many people who believe that there is some kind of vague force, or energy, a higher power, and also that there is some sort of afterlife. In fact, I would venture that the large majority of all people through the ages believe that there is 'something.' What I am saying is that the Bible tells us in detail all about this, and with absolute certainty, not only the history of man in his relations with God, but also the future of man after death. Jesus Himself wanted to completely reassure His disciples. He said that His Father's house has many rooms; that He was going to prepare a place for them. He said, 'If I go and prepare a place for you, I will come back and take you to be with me that you also may be where I am.'"[1]

"All of this is there for us to read," said Richard, "but in the end, we are asked to imagine the unimaginable, aren't we? I mean, we can't really suppose that we can begin to understand God, can we? After

---

[1] John 14:2

all, scientists are just tapping in to try and understand the vastness of the universe, with its extraordinary dimensions and complexity, and yet further beyond that in comprehension is supposed to be a being who made it all. It's beyond us."

"Absolutely, Richard. And those thoughts are expressed in the Bible too. God says, 'As the heavens are higher than the earth, so are my ways higher than your ways and my thoughts than your thoughts.'[2]

"In that sense, God is unknowable. I can't achieve cosmic thinking, as I think you have said. And yet, on the other hand, God has come, in flesh and blood like us, so that we *can* actually know Him.

"In John 14, Jesus said, 'Anyone who has seen me has seen the Father',[3] and again in John 10, His listeners were in no doubt that he was claiming to be God when he said, 'I and the Father are one.'[4] John was quite clear that the Word of God who was the same as God from eternity actually became a human being in Jesus, someone His disciples could sit with, sing a psalm with, and at least in John's case, could lean against Jesus' chest at mealtimes. This Jesus, who said He came down from heaven, and went fishing with them, also told them not to fear death and not to be concerned at His leaving. He told them, and He tells us, that He would still be with them on earth, and they with Him in heaven."

Richard had looked tired, and I wondered if it might be me tiring him, but he said he was fine. "I wonder how many more

---

[2] Isaiah 55:9
[3] John 14:9
[4] John 10:30

conversations we might manage, Bob. I suppose I find it quite hard sometimes to take all this in. I can't achieve cosmic thinking," he said, half-seriously.

"What do you mean?" I asked.

"Well, all of this is one thing, and I wonder if, at some stage, we might talk about what is of great interest to me and that is the Holy Spirit."

I promised Richard that we would definitely do that next time we met.

Chapter 29.

Cosmic Thinking:
Sperm, Ova, and the Holy Spirit

"Having studied embryology, as we doctors all do, the concept that the moment the sperm and ova meet, something immediate and quite remarkable has happened, and goes on being remarkable; as the embryo grows, you are getting mental function as well as physical development."

Richard had jumped straight into where we left off once we had settled down for a chat a few days later, and the small talk about the weather and my work had been completed alongside the now habitual kitchen tea making.

"For me," he continued, "what I have thought from time to time in the past is that maybe there is a recycling; that what comes out of us comes back in the creation of a new life, for example. What is it that happens at the moment of conception that is producing sentient human beings with ideas of morality, and right and wrong? I know that this is probably all nursery stuff to you, Bob. I'm talking about the recycling of energy, and for energy, use the name the Holy Spirit."

"I don't see it as nursery stuff at all, Richard, and you have mentioned things which are indeed a great mystery, and yet explained. I don't see the Holy Spirit in terms of that kind of amorphous energy. The Holy Spirit is a person."

"What!? Say that again," said Richard. "A person?! I have never thought of the Holy Spirit as a person."

"Oh yes, He is the third person of the Trinity. He was there with God, as God, in the beginning. The Spirit of God hovered over the waters right at the beginning of creation. We see His work right through history, empowering and intervening in men's lives, men like Samson or Elijah or Gideon, and bestowing gifts on relative unknowns like Bezalel, son of Uri, who God says He has filled with the Spirit of God 'for wisdom, understanding, knowledge and with all kinds of skills to work in gold, silver, and bronze, to cut and set stones, to work in wood, and to engage in all kinds of crafts'.[1]

"The Holy Spirit is sometimes described as the finger of God, the means by which the vast and unknowable God connects with our human world. Jesus said that if He, by the finger of God cast out demons, then the kingdom of God had come among the people.[2]

"The Spirit of God has always been working and striving with mankind but until the barrier of sin was removed by Jesus, He did not dwell in us. God had breathed spirit into man in the Genesis account of creation and man became a living soul intended to live in union with the Spirit of God. There was loss of that union at the fall, with all the consequences that we still see in our world today, but the Old Testament prophets looked forward, without really

---

[1] Exodus 31:1–6
[2] Luke 11:20

understanding, to the promise of the father; that God Himself would again make a way to dwell with men.

"There was a historical time and place when God did that in Jesus of Nazareth, but Jesus promised His disciples that when He ascended to heaven, the Holy Spirit would come. He also declared that He would come Himself. The 'Father will send the Spirit,' He said, and in the same breath, 'I will come,' and that Jesus and the Father would make their home in those who love Him – 'my Father will love them, and We will make our home with them'. [3]

"There is such interchangeability of roles, which are described in that chapter 14 of John, that we have to conclude the unity of the Trinity, one God, Father, Son and Spirit, all somehow dwelling within the Christian. Elsewhere, the Holy Spirit is called the Spirit of Jesus. He promised that after the resurrection, the Spirit of Jesus Christ, the Spirit of God, the Holy Spirit, all the same person, was going to come and be with them, and in them. That's what happened at Pentecost. If you read chapter two of Acts, Peter describes this promise, the promise of the Spirit being given to all God's people. He was to be poured out on young and old, men and women, and it is this gift of the Holy Spirit, the gift of God Himself, who takes up residence in our hearts and re-connects us with God. It is the Holy Spirit who makes sense of everything, and He is the one who both empowers us for life with God now and secures our future after death.

"I suppose what I'm saying, Richard, is that you can think of the Holy Spirit as Jesus present with you now, though not as the flesh and

---

[3] John 14:23

blood human being that he was. If you can think of Jesus as a person, and I'm sure you can, then you can think of the Holy Spirit as that same person, but not someone who can be touched physically, though he will definitely be happy to come fishing with you. He will walk and talk with you wherever you are; His promise to those who love Him is that He will never leave or forsake us."

"Is that what the Americans call being born again?' asked Richard. "It is, Richard," I said. "And it's also what Jesus Himself called being born again, or variously in other places in the bible, born of God, or born from above. You started with your thoughts about the sperm and ova, and I think you were implying that the ova had nothing much going for it. It had life, if you like, but it was in no way complete. Then, miraculously, at the moment the sperm meets it, a sentient being begins to be formed which becomes human, with all the wonderful attributes of humanity: conscience, morality, and so on. That's not a bad picture of the meaning of being born again.

"Do you remember that Jesus encountered a religious man of His day, a man called Nicodemus, one of the Jewish rulers who sneaks out to see Him at night? You can read about it in John chapter 3. He tells Nicodemus that unless a man is born again, he cannot see or enter the Kingdom of God. Jesus goes on to say that when man procreates, all he can do is make something like himself. Man is physical, made from dust. Jesus explains to Nicodemus that, 'Flesh gives birth to flesh', but he counters that by saying that Spirit, the Holy Spirit, gives birth to the human spirit. Jesus is talking about something similar to the life-giving effect of sperm meeting ova, but He is talking about invisible spiritual things. The result is just as dramatic as what you described between ova and sperm. Those who connect with the Spirit of God become alive in God; they are born again. Immediately, they have new life and grow and develop in spiritual ways that are impossible without that happening.

"That's what I now know happened to me in Norway forty years ago. I now recognise that, before that time, I was spiritually dead and blind. I didn't know that. Someone who is born physically blind does know that he can't see, but it's not the same for the human spirit. When you are spiritually blind, and we are all born that way, Richard, we don't know that our hearts cannot see God and we don't realise that we are born spiritually dead and in darkness. It's the result of our sinful nature, and sin blinds us to God. We have to be reborn with hearts that can see.

"Paul has a prayer for the church in Ephesus that the eyes of their hearts would be able to see the extent of God's love. You will remember John Newton's Amazing Grace, 'I once was blind but now I see.' Do you have a Bible here, Richard?" I asked. "Yes, it's on the shelf in the study," he replied. "Would you mind going to fetch it?" I went a little way down the corridor into Richard's study and ran my finger along the shelves of books but couldn't seem to locate it.

"It's in somewhere with the ones on fly fishing," he called after me from the sofa. Eventually, I found his copy which still looked pretty new, and when I sat down, I located chapter 3 in the gospel of John and read the story of Nicodemus meeting Jesus.

When I had finished, Richard asked, "If you meet born-again Christians, can you recognise their changed state, if I can put it that way?"

"Often, yes," I said. "The Spirit of God has a connection between us and often that is mutually recognised, especially, of course, if we talk about Jesus. But not always. I doubt that anyone would have recognised me as a Christian during my four years of prodigal living. But then, I draw some encouragement that the Bible is full of flawed characters who wander. Just like the prodigal son, they seem to come to their senses and find that their father is eagerly awaiting their return. I didn't behave like a saint in those early years, and often I still don't, but I eventually came to discover that the Bible considered me a saint right from the moment of conception. That's when I became a Christian, not a particularly holy one, I grant you, but nonetheless, all Christians are called saints, Richard.

"It is status and not behaviour that makes me a saint. I'm a child of my father, come what may, once the Spirit places that stamp upon me. Like the embryo, something happened at my spiritual conception, but I am very much a work of God in progress, just as I was when I was first conceived in my mother's womb, placed in a cot when born, figured out how to stick a spoon in my mouth as a youngster, and all the other wonderful stages of human development.

"The Bible calls Christians by many names: children of God; the Bride of Christ; a spiritual Israel; the redeemed of the Lord; all sorts of names, and they are also known as saints, all of them; it is not just those deemed to be special through the human decision of papal beatification.

"Richard, we spoke about how, when we become children of God, our spirits cry out to God as Father. Romans chapter 8 describes all of this; that if we don't have God's Spirit, we are not children of God, but if we do, then we have received the Spirit of sonship and our spirit's cry, 'Abba, Father!' We know and sense that we have been welcomed back to the family home where we truly belong. I am just so grateful that this happened to me when I was 22 years old. But my uncle Francois received the same Spirit when he was 90."

"I hope I've got time left," said Richard.

"While you have breath, you have time, Richard, and I'm convinced that God is with you and shaping you for when you too can say, 'Abba, Father'."

"That's a nice thing to think of. Shall I make you some more tea?"

"I'm alright, Richard," I said, "but before I go away tomorrow, may I pray for you?"

"Yes, please, and I wonder if your prayer might include some reference to my healing as well. Is that alright? I was going to say I don't expect miracles, but you have seen the x-ray."

I laid my hands on Richard's arm again and prayed and gave thanks for the evidence of healing thus far on his x-ray, and I prayed to the One who also knows the x-ray of our souls that He would reveal to Richard his own great love for him.

"Thank you, Bob, I am very grateful."

"I am grateful too, for our friendship, and for the joy of this journey that we have embarked upon together. Perhaps I can leave you with this thought. When you hang around with the right company, you are more likely to become like them. The opposite is also true - bad company corrupts. Jesus may have left this earth, but He sent His Spirit and if we are intent on walking closely with Him, we are more likely to become as He is. There's a limit to that, of course. Hanging around with Einstein wouldn't have made me a genius. But it's different with the Holy Spirit; He not only teaches, guides, and encourages us, He also empowers us.

"Where we may have lacked the ability to understand, or the power to kick a bad habit, or the courage to speak out and confront wrongdoing, the Holy Spirit empowers us for Christian life. That same power that raised Jesus from the dead is going to raise me from death, and, on occasions, do things like heal your broken arm when I pray. For now, though, the Holy Spirit is the One who helps us to experience God's heart, His love for us. He is the One who gives us God's hug.

"I suppose being a Christian can largely be summed up by that one thing, Richard: knowing the closeness of God's hug, Christ within us, and also in all those who receive Him by faith."

Chapter 30.

Sophie

I left Richard that morning with a profound sense of expectation that God was going to do something, but I was also worried that perhaps I should have grabbed more opportunity. I knew that all this talking would not in itself bring about the awakening in Richard that I was hoping to see, but I also knew that the journey we were on together was just that, a journey; it was up to God which corner or crossroads would be the one where they would meet. My mind went back to other opportunities, journeys of expectation and hope where, in the end, there was only suffering and there were no answers, at least not in this life.

The last time I had seen my niece, Sophie, one of my younger brother Andrew's four daughters, it was in the French Alps where the family lives. She was coming to an age where, for the first time, we clicked with banter and chat, and for a while, we had such great fun, speaking in pretend languages, using the kind of words, intonations, and gestures that an Italian, or a Norwegian, or a Russian, might use, without us actually knowing the language. She was particularly good at it, and we had a lot of laughter for a few minutes while playing that game together in front of our amused families.

A few years earlier, when she was perhaps ten or eleven, and we were at lunch in my brother's chalet, Sophie had suddenly asked a question: "What is a god?" Before I had even begun to collect my thoughts, someone moved the conversation on, and Sophie was never answered.

My son Jack was the same age as Sophie and they were good friends, mostly on Facebook either side of visits. She was a really lively and a very lovely girl. Not long after our trip, I came home from work one evening and Enid wasn't there, and I thought I would check for messages on the telephone. There was one from my mother. She sounded very distressed, and the message just said, 'Bob, Sophie's been killed!'

It took a few moments to take in what her message said, and then I couldn't really believe what I had heard. I thought, surely I'm not hearing the message right. Mum must surely have mixed her words; she sometimes got things a bit mixed up. But when I called my mother straight back and she had picked up the phone, it became clear through her tears and trembling voice that Sophie had indeed died.

It was news that Mum had heard from my older brother Tony that morning. There had been a call from France the morning after we all visited Brighton for Tony's 60th birthday. The call came while Andrew was out jogging and his niece Helen had been the one to tell him, when he arrived back from his run, that his daughter had died.

Sophie was fifteen. It seems that she had snuck out of the family home in Châtel, in the French Alps, just the other side of the Swiss border, and she had gone to a party in one of the neighbouring villages. No one had even known she wasn't in her bed. At the end of the party, she had been reluctant to accept a ride home from a French boy, but in the end, she was persuaded, along with two other girls. The picture wasn't at all clear at first, but later, we came to know that they weren't drinking. It had been a cold night, the car heater was on, and the driver fell asleep. He drove into a brick culvert by the side of the mountain road. Sophie was the only one who died, while one of the other girls held her hand, though there were other life-changing injuries to another girl.

By the time Enid and I and our son Jack had arrived in France, our daughter Lydia and other members of the wider family were already there. We had raced to get my mother a passport but, in the end, medical advice did not allow her to travel. There was profound shock and grief amongst the whole family, and indeed, throughout the local French villages. The whole area was affected, not least because it seemed that the young driver was the fire chief's son.

Sophie's body lay in the chambre funéraire, located between villages, and she was laid out in a private viewing room. Her parents and two of the older sisters had already visited her body before we arrived and it was arranged that we should go with her mother's brother, and also that we should take her youngest sister, who was about six years old. This was something much more customary in France than in the UK.

When we arrived at the funeral home, we waited a few minutes for the door to the viewing room to be unlocked, and to be shown in. Sophie was laid on a bed, dressed in her clothes and with embalming makeup. It didn't really look like the Sophie we had known, who was so full of life and laughter. We just stood there, the five of us, and no one said a word for ages. No one knew what to say, and the only movement was when her youngest sister reached for her uncle's hand.

I suggested that it might be better for those that wanted if we went out and came back in again alone. I thought that perhaps it might be better that way, if we did want to say something to Sophie, though I had not experienced shock and grief so intensely numbing as this before. I really didn't know what I was supposed to be thinking or doing. None of us did.

We did go back in alone, my son Jack too, though her sister Naomi went in with her uncle. I don't know what was said and I can't remember what I said, if anything. It was the same when we brothers and her uncle later went to the crematorium to see her coffin off. No one else wanted to come and we sat there for quite a while, in front of the coffin, before it was to be removed for cremation. No one could say anything.

Older brother Tony had suggested that perhaps I should say a few words. I suppose he was thinking that, as the only religious one in the family, I might know what to say. But my head was still bowed, and I shook it to indicate no, I didn't feel I could say anything at all that would begin to meet our sorrow or comfort my brother for the loss of his lovely daughter.

The funeral was crowded. The whole town came, as well as very many teenagers from the surrounding schools which had closed for the day. The street passing through one side of the village square was blocked off and use of the large town hall had been donated to my brother's family by the local mayor and municipality. It seems that this Anglo-French tragedy, together with the fire chief's connection, meant that the whole area was shut down for this funeral.

None of my family had church connections, and France is very secular. It had been agreed by my brother and his wife that they would ask me to do something of the 'God bit', to 'say a prayer or something'. The town hall was packed, and I don't know how the family managed to get through the service, which was attended by hundreds. The least injured person from the accident was also there, with a cast on his arm. I think he was the driver but I'm not sure. I sought him out afterwards and said hello, but my French is not good enough for what would have been a difficult conversation even in English.

Sophie's older sister, Jennifer, was prepared to say her piece, but she froze and could not get up to speak at the funeral. The next time I saw her, in Brighton quite a while later, I noticed that she had a tattoo. It was something her parents would never have allowed and so it was under the hairline on the nape of her neck and was beautifully done in script. It simply said, *'wake her up and tell her I love her.'*

Fifteen years later, I noticed the same thing, a tattoo with different words on Jennifer's younger sister, revealed on the nape of her neck when her hair was drawn up. Both were private eulogies for such a profound and sudden loss.

With great difficulty in retaining composure, I had closed the funeral addresses that day with just a few words; with an apology from my mother, Sophie's granny, for not being able to come, and with prayer. After the reception, the family was given space in the street outside. The attending crowd spilled out of the town hall and filled the square, which looked out over the mountains, and a private space was cordoned in the street just for the family.

Some Chinese lanterns had been brought from England. We lit fifteen of them as the villagers watched, and they floated slowly up towards the mountains before disappearing. Later, when it was dark, we lit fifteen more from the chalet down in the valley, and I expect there were many in the village above who again saw them rise into the night sky.

There have been many times since when I have wondered what more I might have said or done, but there are just no answers this side of heaven. I will have to wait until then for more to be revealed. In the meantime, I am acutely conscious about not finding the opportunity to reach out to my family in a way that I now feel I should have done. I am grateful that my brother's reading of this book many years later gave us that opportunity to talk.

Chapter 31.

Richard's Wretched Feet

Whenever we met again, at some point in our conversation, Richard brought up what he called his miraculous recovery. Within a very short time of the bone beginning to lay down across the break, his arm had grown strong, and he was able to practice casting a fly in the open parking square of his gated complex. It was without a hook, I imagine, but nonetheless, casting his line back and forth so soon after his arm had been severely broken was indeed a miracle.

He would say things like, "I can assure you, Bob, without a shadow of a doubt, my surgeon and physio are quite astounded. And so am I. I didn't think I would be able to fish again, but as far as I'm concerned, I'm healed and back in action."

On one occasion, he brought up the reminder, and with considerable seriousness, he added a more recent experience. "I don't know what you think of this, Bob. I would value your opinion. I was leaving church the other day and was in conversation with someone we both know as I walked out the doorway. We were talking about this arm, and he told me that he had suffered from quite serious pain in their shoulder and arm for fifteen years. I put out a sympathetic hand and touched him, nothing more than that, and do you know, he called me the next day to say that his pain had completely gone, after fifteen years! Now, what do you think of that? Do you think I might have got the healing touch like you? I mean, it seems to me to be beyond coincidence. I can't really fathom it. What do you think?"

"Richard, I don't know what to think. God does things the way He wants to, and when He wants to, and we often can't fathom it. I know that healing is a gift from Him. He is the one who heals and since it is a gift it's not something that originates from us, or something we possess. It's not as though *I* have become a healer, or *you* have become a healer, though there are certainly those through whom He more frequently grants gifts of healing for others. We don't have 'healing hands', as some people say. God alone is the One who heals us, but He may indeed have chosen your own circumstances, and your touch that morning, to be a channel for that healing to your friend. I certainly wouldn't discount it, but we probably won't know for sure. I am, of course, pleased for him, and also that it has stimulated your excitement and your faith, and that you seem to be fighting fit again."

In December 2017, the birth of our daughter's baby was approaching, and we had decided to take an extended break to be near her in Ibiza for the birth. I had tried to squeeze in another visit to see Richard but didn't make it in the end, and though it was nagging me just to give him a call, that too was neglected.

When we got back at the beginning of the New Year, I had a message cancelling an appointment with Richard. He wasn't feeling too well, and I thought he didn't sound so great in the message he had left, but I had been away and needed to catch up at work and I failed to follow up. Eventually, I heard from his first wife, Mary, that Richard was in hospital. He had fallen and had already been in the West Middlesex for a while.

Enid and I went to visit as soon as we could and found him in reasonably good form. He filled the bed very generously from head to foot. A few toes were sticking out, exposed at the end of his blanket, and we could see with some concern that they were black, or more like the colour of an aubergine, a purple-black, and grossly swollen.

"Richard!" I had called as we approached his bed, and he opened his eyes. "Bob, Enid. Hello! I'm so glad to see you both." His voice was slightly slurred and sounding tired. "You're in a stroke ward, Richard!" We drew up some chairs and asked what had been going on. "Oh, they play solitaire with the beds here. They must have a particularly good computer system because they are forever shifting people around. A bed becomes vacant and half an hour later there's a new patient in it. I've been in three wards since I came but I think I'm being downgraded now to something not quite so intensive."

"Your left foot looks a bit sunburnt," I said, not wishing to be too accurate. "You can see why I am here. My wretched feet! Pull up the sheet and you can see the full horror." We pulled the sheet back from his legs and both Enid and I gasped. Both his legs were grossly swollen and so discoloured.

"I must have mentioned to you in the past, Bob, that I suffer from this infected eczema on my legs. I get bouts of it every three or four months, or something like that, and the GP gives me a week of antibiotics. Usually, it's troublesome, it flares up, it debilitates me, I get weakened and a bit shaky. But over the last year or more, it hasn't really been responding to treatment.

"This bout started on a Sunday, I think, and I went to bed early feeling very shaky and really was only half in bed. I sort of fell across the bed, you know, couldn't be bothered. Very early on Monday morning, I was feeling a bit chilly, so I thought, 'Come on, Richard, straighten up and put your pyjamas on'. I swung back and sat on the bed and put on the left leg of my pyjama trousers and the right leg was sort of spiralled. When you're debilitated, the least little thing becomes almost insuperable. Things which are so trivial, you know; I couldn't untangle this *bloody* thing, so I thought I would stand up and as I stand up, it will straighten up and I'll slide my leg out. Well, it didn't. I sort of half got it down and with the effort of doing what I was doing, I just fell down. Being me, when I fall, I fall. So, I went down with a hell of a bang.

"That was about 2 am on Monday morning, and there I was, flat on my back. Now, I've got awfully nice neighbours, but I didn't hear any movement until about 8 am on Wednesday, so I was on the floor for about 28, no, 30 hours. I literally could not move. I had terrific pain in both hips. I thought, Rondel, you've certainly fractured at least one of them. I lay there and thought beautiful thoughts for hours and hours and hours. I couldn't get to my telephone because I was on the floor and anything on the table was out of reach.

"I'm boring you." "No, no, Richard. I'm horrified," Enid said. "And I'm so sorry we didn't call, Richard," I added. I had had that message from Richard, presumably not long before the fall, and now I was mortified that I had been too busy. My friend could have died alone while I was going about my business. The thought was too troubling

"Well, people have said, what about your family? Didn't they check up? But families don't call every day. There was no reason. You don't need to apologise." Richard changed tack. "Now actually, Bob, does Enid know about this fracture, what happened with my arm and how rapidly it healed?" It seemed that perhaps Richard was asking for the jam again, without actually asking.

"Yes, Richard, and we will pray now if you would like. We have come with that in mind." "I was praying for that," said Richard. "I really, really would appreciate it. I'm so glad you've come." There was a sense of relief in his voice, and we could see that this dear man must have had a pretty dreadful time. "We will do that before we go, but we are not about to run now. We'll do that shortly."

We had brought out some strawberries and bits and pieces and treats for him. "Oh, how kind! Trout and Salmon!" I had brought a fishing magazine for him. "Yes, you can do a bit of escapism if you can't go fishing. I hope you like strawberries."

"Yes, I love them. Look, for now, I'll put it all amongst my array of bottles. Ever since I arrived, I've been peeing like a fire engine." Richard then continued his account of the fall. "Anyway, I lay there for ages thinking someone must call by, or something, but they didn't. Fortunately, a neighbour called in; the door is often unlocked, as you know. She found me and got me in here. I think I just had a few hours, and it would have been my funeral you were attending. As you can see, my legs have got badly infected, and they are trying to get to grips with that with antibiotics. But enough of me, what about you? Any news?"

"Richard, we're so sorry to see you like this. And I'm so sorry I didn't get to drop in before we went away. Yes, we have a beautiful grandson, but chat about all of that can wait. It was your Mary that called me to let us know. I think she must have picked up a message."

"Oh, you didn't get to meet her I don't think. She's been an absolute brick. Two days before this happened, she has a cousin up in Rutland who is 96 and who fell and fractured his femur, and she's been up there looking after him and had just got back from that when Rondel got up to his old tricks."

"Richard," I said, "You're so far up in the clouds that when you do fall, you would have thought you would have time to think about what's happening." We laughed and talked about what help he would need, and we went to the hospital shop for earplugs and a few bits and pieces. Shortly after returning, he mentioned that his son Mark might be coming any moment and perhaps Enid and I would pray for him beforehand. He thought we might draw the bed curtains, which we did, and we prayed for him just before leaving, and for his poor legs, and we left just as his son and family were coming down the corridor to visit.

Richard recovered well and was soon back home. He even managed another fishing trip or two in the Spring, but that incident wasn't his only fall. When I met him at his front door again, he looked as though he had applied commando camouflage. There was a large black stripe on his forehead and another above his right eyebrow and various other smaller marks about his face.

"Oh, these are carpet burns," he explained. "I'm such an idiot! I had dropped a coin at this door when I was coming in. It turned out to be just a penny. The door was unlocked as I bent down to pick it up and I just sort of kept on going, like a felled tree, I suppose, and just as big. My head hit the front door which swung back and then my face slid along the carpet as I straightened out, hence these burn scabs. The door rammed the wall with great force - you can see the dent the knob has made - and then it sprung back and clonked me on top of my head. I'm OK. I think I must look a bit like a Red Indian painted up for war."

"You do indeed, Richard." I was sympathetically amused at his appearance, but his main concern was the door. He had hit it so hard that it had sprung the hinges and would no longer close.

"Do you know a chap who can fix this, Bob? Nothing too expensive."

"I think I do, Richard. Have you got a screwdriver? Not a Philips, these are ordinary slot-head screws." Richard rooted around in his study and came back with one. I tightened the screws into the frame and the door then closed perfectly. "No charge! Except a cup of tea and maybe a chocolate biscuit - or two?"

"Splendid!" Richard said. "Well done. Let's get the kettle on. Perhaps you wouldn't mind brewing for us this time so I can rest my legs." He often wore his boxer shorts around the house, and I could see that his legs were heavily bandaged above his sandals.

Once we had settled in his living room with the usual small plate of chocolate biscuits and a cup of tea, Richard opened with, "I've had an epiphany, Bob!" It grabbed my attention.

"Bob, I think I've overstayed my welcome." I was puzzled. "What do you mean?" "I have days when I think it's all dragging on a bit," Richard continued. "The challenge is finding something to do that justifies the gift of being here. I toddle on down to St Mary's on Sundays and say, 'what do you want me to do next?', you know. Sometimes I go and look at my old files to remind myself that there was a time when I was living an enormously busy life. You forget it. But when I do remember, I sort of think, what am I doing here now?

"I realise that I can no longer do the things that I used to do. I had thought that I would stop fishing at the end of this year. But It's too risky. When I was last at Ashmere Lakes, I fell down and it took two big men to pick me up. So, even if I go with one partner and I fall, it's too risky. If I went in the water, that would be that. I'm finding it quite important to think about where to park the car. I'm on fairly heavy doses of diuretics and antihistamine. I have to think more of logistics. So, I'm going to pack it in now."

I had thought that Richard's epiphany was going to be about a spiritual encounter, or at least something revelatory along those lines. It was revelatory for him, though mildly deflating for me, and I'm sure also disappointing for him. He was sounding wistful and mildly depressed. Fishing was the love of his life, one of Richard's few remaining expeditionary pleasures, and although he said all this pretty matter-of-factly, I knew it must have been a significant and rather sad milestone for him. We were both quiet for a minute and there was a knock at the door.

Richard asked if I would mind answering. It was a courier delivering a large plastic bag with a box inside. "Looks like shoes, Richard. Size fifteen?" "No. Size seventeen." "Seventeen?!" I queried.

"Yes, they have swollen, and I can't get my size fifteens on anymore. They have a special lymphoedema clinic which I go to for what I've got. I've been putting up with this now for several years, but this series of bandages will be off and on for four weeks in various ways. At first, they were so bulky I couldn't get any footwear on at all, but I've cut these sandals to bits and lengthened them with Velcro.

Rather clever, I think, otherwise I wouldn't be able to get out at all. Sitting around like this gets quite hard. I have to work very hard to fill the hours through the day. I do crosswords to keep my brain going, and I do calligraphy. I've started to play the ukulele. I used to play the violin, I don't know if I told you that, and I do something on Mondays called Man with a Pan, cooking organised by Age UK, and I've done a six-week course in conversational French."

"But no more fishing, dear Richard, no more fishing. We will have to live in our memories for that. Did I ever tell you my most exciting fishing tale, Richard? I don't think I did."

Chapter 32.

Lockdown

I recounted a fishing tale to Richard with great nostalgia. It was the story of a marlin that got away when I went out with a boatman off the coast of Panama and Costa Rica, where my daughter was living for a few years. This fishing story was to be the last for a long time.

2019 became an exceptionally busy year and I somehow managed to get sepsis in August which could easily have been the end of everything. By October, I had recovered sufficiently, and Enid and I had long planned a break to visit friends in Hong Kong and New Zealand. It was a splendid trip and just before going, I printed a draft manuscript of our book. I asked Richard if he would review it for my return in early January. This was something he was pleased to do since he had not yet seen a single sentence written.

On my return, I was feeling nervous about his reaction. Besides attending to neglected business, I suppose I put off an early visit for a week or two, but I bumped into Richard heading to Waitrose one morning. "Richard!" "Bob!" Richard always elongated the 'o' in Bob. It was emphatic and affectionate. His speech was nearly always animated, never flat, and some words in most sentences were given strong vowel emphasis, in tune with his enthusiastic manner in all our conversations. "Borrrb! How nice to *see* you!"

We chatted a bit about the trip, and this and that, and I then asked if he had read the manuscript. "Yes!" he said, seemingly with some enthusiasm. "Twice, in fact, and I have a file of notes. Come over and we'll run through them. There are some bits – I think I've told you before that I have never spoken to anyone – there are some bits that I might want to abstract. In the past few years, I've sort of regained a certain balance in the family that was destroyed when I left, and so there is stuff in there that may set us back. Nothing that I've said that I regret, but I wouldn't want to spoil that. The rest of it is what I call routine editorial. That is where I am, Bob. So how are we on a time frame?"

"Let's make a date then, Richard. We are out to Spain again to visit our daughter for my birthday, so when we come back, say mid-Feb?"

I didn't get to make that date. We had another short weekend trip to Dublin early in March for a meeting Enid needed to attend for her work with the Nepal Leprosy Trust. I went along so that we could both see the good friends we had stayed with in New Zealand who had relocated there.

On the last day in Dublin, I had noticed Enid had a slight cough. The airport was practically deserted when we flew home on Monday 9th March in the evening and the prospect of a Covid-19 lockdown was on the horizon. Enid grew progressively unwell that week, and worse still the following, with a fever and cough. It seemed likely that she had Covid, though medical help was useless as the whole country descended into that first lockdown, with the accompanying hospital pressures and high mortality.

After four weeks, Enid was really struggling. She should have gone into hospital, but she had a phobia of hospitals from childhood, and we had both heard enough on the news to know that if she went in, it might have been the last time we saw each other, through closing ambulance doors. No visiting would have been allowed and so my son and I both nursed her, forcing down liquids and vitamins and making endless orange juice lollies to keep her mouth and airways relieved with some moisture. It was about the only thing she could tolerate through several weeks of desperate coughing and sleepless nights until she eventually began to surface around late April, though with extreme weakness and with later hair loss.

Now aged 88, Richard was off-limits for months except for phone calls. Eventually, Enid did mostly recover, and Richard did manage a tea in August, socially distanced in our small garden, but he forgot to bring his file of notes. However, by October 2020, he was happy enough for me to introduce him to a lady's sewing group almost on his doorstep, and to resume my visits to his flat as lockdown measures eased. All his calligraphy and weaving and church visits had more or less stopped since March and he was struggling with loneliness outside of family visits, which were mostly at weekends.

"Sit where it's comfortable. There are too many cushions there; it's the interior decorator, piling them high. Would you like a biscuit?" Richard still had a packet of chocolate digestive biscuits for our tea.

"To tell you the truth, Richard, I rang your bell earlier and left again. There must have been a mix-up with our time. I was halfway back to the car when I thought, what if Richard has fallen, lying somewhere unable to move, and so, I let myself in and had a nose around." Richard still left his flat key in the lock even if no visitors were expected. It was a gated complex with a common entry door to his block and he felt safe to do that.

"I was checking on you, Richard. Hope you don't mind. And then you responded later to my phone message, and I had time to come back."

"I had my mobile but didn't look at it in the middle of Waitrose. It's good that you do check, Bob, absolutely."

Richard was nearly always without his trousers indoors. He wore a fairly massive pair of navy-blue boxers and his feet, right up to the knees, were encased in tight flesh-coloured compression bandages.

"Your legs are looking alright, Richard." "Yes, they are, but I'm in these stockings 24/7. If I leave them off for 24 hours, boof! They swell up and I can't get shoes on, and you've seen me with my size seventeens, the largest I can get, from America, so any swelling and that's it. The stockings are on for life.

"Now, I've seen your Facebook, Bob. You've been busy. There's a thing in physics called the Brownian Motion, where all the atoms in a fluid are moving in all directions, like Baron Munchausen, riding off in all directions!"

That image seemed to just about sum me up, and to add credence, I veered off into another direction. "I'd like to progress the writing, Richard. I haven't looked at it for a while."

"Will you be adding to it?" he asked.

"I might build in some of my poetry at the end, or somewhere, but I want to get cracking on it."

The one thing I had never told Richard was that I didn't expect to end the book until he died, whenever that might be. He might have realised, but despite the closeness of our relationship, I never fully explored with him that I was looking and praying for the reassurance of his salvation. The ending, and its timing, was something I had to leave in God's hands.

"I'll look at it again over the weekend," he said. "Come at 11 on Monday and we can make a start, though it will take us to lunchtime. I don't lunch, normally. I am just hunkered down. I go out to shop at Waitrose, and I do a walk whenever I can. I need the exercise. I have never had so many books on my table. I just read, and the other thing I do…," Richard hesitated just a little, "and I confess this to you, Bob, I am drinking a lot. It helps. It helps in the evenings, not during the day, particularly now the nights are drawing in; when you are on your own, they are long. They are awfully long," He spoke slowly and wistfully. "So, we are all coping in whatever ways we can. Anyone I talk to who is living alone has the same trouble, Bob - this wretched virus. Trying to fill the days intelligently is difficult. Crosswords galore, all that mundane stuff, but there are days when it doesn't work and it's difficult, very difficult. But I'm comfortable…."

I could hear the sadness in Richard's voice. The pandemic had increased isolation for so many and I felt for him. "My father got into that," I said. "He drank late in life until he died at 85. Mostly, he forgot that he had poured a morning whisky and so then had another, and another."

"I'm nearly 89, Bob. It's four years since that 85th party. The church has been doing what it can - Zooming for England! But I just can't do it. There's a little service open on a Wednesday morning which I've always loved but I have to tell you, Bob, when I go into church now, all I can think of is what the hell am I still doing here? I don't mean that to sound flippant. It's not a very positive thought. I miss the people, and this wretched Covid has put me all on my own."

"Oh, Richard, it is wretched, isn't it? The church is all about people. It's not the pulpit and the pews or the stained glass, as nice as they might be. It's the company of fellow believers and the encouragement of those you love and who love you. We're a strange bunch, aren't we? Mostly, it's people we would never otherwise meet, from all walks of life, everyone with our own journeys and our wounds that need healing. I am certain that I would be a sad and grumpy divorcee, several times over perhaps, if it were not for the fact that Jesus put me in His family of oddballs and misfits in need of grace and love. They have been an instrument for changing me and keeping me on the right track. We can annoy and irritate each other like any family, and just like any family, it's where the love is deepest that wounding is also most deep, but there is nothing like it to learn to grow in compassion, patience, humility, and most of all love. Anyway, the church of God's people is God's idea, and a pretty good one"

"I miss it," said Richard, "but I just can't get by with masks, fist bumps and Zoom screens. My prayer, and I pray a lot now, my prayer is that I would be given guidance to use the extra years well, to make a difference - not the right word - to do what I can, to be useful, I don't know. I pray for guidance to live as the Lord would wish me to live."

We met again as planned on the following Monday. Richard produced a yellow ring-bound file and showed it to me. "Those are my annotations which we can talk about. Others are simple editing content. I'll boil the kettle, hold on."

Richard disappeared to make morning coffee and find the customary biscuits. When he came back, he saw me looking at a photo on his window ledge. He was standing by himself at the front of a flat-bottomed boat, like a punt, on a dead calm azure sea, bent rod in hand and the boatman at the other end of the boat. Some animation came back to his voice.

"The Yucatan peninsula. The tarpon nursery. Up further to the north, they get bigger, a hundred, hundred and ten pounds. I've caught a hundred-and-ten-pound tarpon in Florida, and it was a struggle. A female, and I suppose we worked it for just under 30 minutes. You see that trophy photograph with the bloke standing waist-deep in water. This thing was so big we couldn't boat it and so we just had to take a picture of it alongside the boat. I caught that on mullet, but the smaller ones are more fun, to be honest. You have to sort of try and winch that size in and I'm not sure it's sport anymore."

"I know. My tussle with a 400 lb marlin, as estimated by the boatman in his small skiff, though I'm not so sure it was that big, that struggle was not so much fun as a complete drama. I really though the small boat could get capsized. We could have cut the line, of course, if we had had something to hand to do that with, or I could have ditched the rod, but what fisherman does that?"

Richard had two Clive James poetry compilations on his coffee table and as I noticed them, I remarked in surprise that I was about to buy them, following a friend's recommendation just the previous Sunday.

"I can get to Waterstones on Wednesday," he said. "Let me buy them for you." We spoke for a while about poetry and, having his file in my hand, I managed to quickly find the page where I had matched him with the farrier in Gerard Manly Hopkins' poem, and I read those lines aloud: 'big-boned and hardy-handsome'. Richard mentioned one of his favourite poems: In the Harbour: Loss and Gain by Longfellow. I brought it up on Google and read aloud:

When I compare What I have lost with what I have gained, What I have missed with what attained, Little room do I find for pride. I am aware How many days have been idly spent; How like an arrow the good intent Has fallen short or been turned aside. But who shall dare To measure loss and gain in this wise? Defeat may be victory in disguise; The lowest ebb is the turn of the tide.

"I'm very privileged," he said somewhat wistfully. "I need that sort of thing now, Bob. Living alone, it is very difficult to resist sequences of negative thought. All those thoughts of good intent falling short just come in. I am hoping for the turning of the tide.

"I retired in 2003, seventeen years ago, and the medicine that I knew no longer exists. I have trouble remembering that I ever did anything good, and I don't think that's just me, I think perhaps it's the same for a lot of old people. I need to be reminded occasionally that I did actually do one or two things that were quite good. But there's no one now to do that for me, no one. The kids don't really know that much about me and perhaps that's common in a lot of families, though my daughter has now chosen to encourage me to talk to her about my life."

"It's a phase of life which I am just beginning, Richard. You gradually slide out of being the chief honcho and new people don't even know what you did. You were somebody, and then, eventually, you're nobody."

Richard continued to reminisce. "There were two doctors who were part of my medical life, Peter Stonier, who lives in the Retreat nearby, and Brian Genery. Both of them I relate to by what we did at Surrey, and they are the only two people left who know anything about me. It can sometimes be quite hard to live with that. You begin to wonder if you have been fooling yourself. You know, I wasn't really that much of a deal. There are some who have a great core of strength, but I don't have that."

"Perhaps this is more of a man's problem," I said, "because we are more focused on achievement than relationship. We are more 'doers', and we derive our esteem from that. The fading of all that is a phase of life that I am now just beginning to recognise. I'm looking at the prospect in a year or two of going into the place of work that I founded and some of the people there, staff and volunteers, won't know me from Adam. They will ask me how they can help. Do I need a shower or the foodbank?!"

Richard then started to recount something I hadn't known about him. He was recognised as one of the founding fathers of contemporary pharmaceutical medicine and its global development and regulation. With his wife, Mary, he had also founded a company to teach doctors the efficacy of clinical trials and he wrote authoritatively on global clinical data management as the digital world began to develop. The second edition of his book on this subject still retails at over £200.

"In 1970, somewhere about then, I and two of my colleagues, Bill Burland and Jan Jouhar, sat in a pub in Wigmore Street and we took a decision to start a new movement which today is the International Federation of Associations of Pharmaceutical Physicians. It's known as IFAPP. It was all about developing international collaboration and coordination of pharmaceutical medicine and the development of medicine worldwide. We had the patronage of Prince Philip, and I was president from 1978 to 1981. It now has establishments in thirty-five countries. I suppose IFAPP has had considerable influence globally in the field of pharmaceutical medicine, including, of course, the current pandemic. But my two colleagues are long dead, and nobody knows me now. Without Bill, Jan, and me, that would never have happened."

"Richard, I am now recognising this as part of the human condition. It's that age we reach when our achievements are mostly behind us. Nonetheless, those of us with faith recognise that the preparation for eternity continues, and that our esteem is not built only on our worldly achievements, over what is really a fleeting span, but on our eternal relationship with our creator. To be honest, Richard, I think that God's greatest concern is not what we might do for Him in this life.

"I mean, God's ability to achieve his purposes doesn't drop through the floor because we fail, or go off track here and there, or come to a rather whimpering end in what the world considers to have been a useful life. I am sure that God is more concerned about what He does *in* us. It's that scripture that again comes to mind which says that we are firstly God's workmanship, created in Christ Jesus in order to do the good works that He has planned for us. His work *in* us comes first and foremost, and it doesn't end at 70 or 90 or 110, or whatever our allotted span may be. Our work in this world that really counts only follows from his work in us. We can't do anything without Him and it's only His work that truly lasts to eternity. The Bible calls His work in us our sanctification. We are being shaped as saints bring Him glory, and in that shaping to enjoy an eternal relationship with Him. Not only that, but we are due to rule and reign with Him in afterlife. We are most definitely not going to be sitting in heavenly deckchairs strumming harps forever and a day. I can't think of anything duller. No, our life will continue with an even greater purpose than this one"

"I haven't talked with you like this for a long time, Bob. I know you thought I was 87. We must have missed nearly two years, and it's probably nearly two years since we last got down to it. I can say that being given these extra years is a responsibility, not to waste it. Perhaps I should reflect on that poem that He's still trying to write in me rather than my rather meagre scratchings from what is now a past life."

Chapter 33.

A & E

Richard had been persuaded by his GP to get his heart checked and, against his better judgement, it led to what should have been a brief spell in hospital to have a pacemaker fitted, but I heard that something had gone wrong. I managed to connect with one call while he was at home after the procedure, but he was so fed up, angry even, that he didn't want to talk, and he was clearly in a lot of pain. I had gathered that the procedure had been messed up and had punctured his pericardium, which had then filled with fluid. He was somewhat despairing that he could ever recover and was very annoyed that he had to face a lot of visits to drain the fluid and redo the procedure. It was all a bit much for an 89-year-old and brought him considerable discomfort and worry. Richard was miserable and wanted to be left alone. I had never known him like this in our nearly six years of friendship.

By the time I got to see him face to face about three weeks later, on the morning of February 26th, I was anticipating some doom and gloom but was able to comment that he was looking ok, and much better than I had expected.

"Everything is fine! I hate to say it ... Hubris! Chocolate biscuits? Remind me, milk and sugar with your coffee?"

Richard told me briefly about his heart problem and raged about the medical incompetence that had led to his discomfort, and what he had felt at one point would be the end of him. He had woken at 4 am with quite severe abdominal pain and thought he was getting another bout of his pericarditis. He got down to his GP that afternoon and went in to be examined, which he marvelled at since it wasn't usual to get an examination anymore, and certainly not during Covid. He had then been packed off to hospital and it turned out that one of the pacemaker leads had punctured his pericardium leading to those several weeks of pain and discomfort.

It had taken a while to sort out but now he was now his usual and very animated self and our conversation turned to Clive James and his poetry. "I found his last volumes very convincing, but sad in a way," Richard said. "How his life had disintegrated in the end, with an expected death that seemed to be a long time in coming. I read one of the obituaries and I think he was more or less reconciled with his wife."

Richard had been down to Waterstones and bought me two of Clive James volumes which he handed over and hoped very much that I would enjoy them.

"I can't blame Covid entirely, but everything is now on Zoom." He continued. "My church gets more participation now than they did in the pews, but I can't get on with it, and I've sort of lost touch with the church, Bob. I find that very distressing. I don't know what to do about it. I'm hoping that once things open up and we get an ordinary communion..." he tailed off in thought. ".. but when the celebrant has a plastic visor on and you can only take a wafer, you know, it's not for me. I find it very distressing," he said again, and as he began to reflect, his buoyant mood had quickly changed after our initial greeting.

"Perhaps I'm being too superficial. I mean, I don't worry about the Church of England, but I do worry about me! You are different from me, Bob, in that you practice your religion in a different way. I have in the past felt quite strongly about my connection with my religious belief and practice and devotion - I'm just hanging on to that now as it's in shreds. It's very distressing."

I had not often seen Richard depressed but there was an air of depression about him, and he was expressing his loneliness. "I am glad you have come today. I can't talk about this to anyone else."

I asked Richard if he had heard the story about the young man and the coal fire. He hadn't, and so I proceeded to tell Richard about a young man who had visited an older friend and similarly expressed the sense of loss. His faith had gone cold and there no longer seemed to be any spark within. The older man had listened patiently, saying nothing until the young friend had finished pouring out his heart. Without a word, the old man simply reached for the fire tongs and took a lump of coal out of the fire to place it on the hearth beside them and they both watched as the burning coal soon lost its brightness. The heat and orange glow faded to black, at which point the old man placed the coal back into the midst of the other coals where it soon began to burn brightly again.

"We need the warmth of the church, Richard. It's part of God's design that we keep warm together. Outside of it, we can easily grow cold. Church has always been the people of God communing with him together. There is hope, Richard. You will be restored when God's people are able to congregate and worship together again."

"So, you are telling me it will come back? You know me well, Bob. I believe it will come back. It's not that I feel deserted. It's the other way round. I feel as though I'm deserting the church. I just don't feel His presence like I sometimes used to. "

"No, but he is present, Richard." I tried to reassure him. "The loss of feeling of His presence is not necessarily a sign of His absence. There are seasons of suffering. There are even places in the Bible that mention the Lord withdrawing His Spirit from someone to see how they will respond. In seasons of difficulty, our faith is made stronger, but He will never leave His children. Never."

"I hope it doesn't sound as though I'm lamenting, Bob, but nice to talk about it. I have been well for years and apart from this heart thing, I am well now, and I treasure that."

I didn't see Richard for a few more weeks. I had heard via a mutual friend of his that he hadn't been well again, and then I got a text from my wife on the morning of March 29th: 'Bob, just spoken to Joy, and Richard has been ill for a week. Tummy upset and bronchial pneumonia. He hasn't wanted Joy to visit but she feels he might see you.'

I called Richard's house phone pretty much straight away and he picked up. He was very breathless and rasping. "Richard! you don't sound at all well."

"Oh, Bob, I've had enough. I'm about to get a taxi to take me to A & E." "I'll take you. Which hospital?" "Middlesex." "I'll be there in five minutes." "Make it ten," he said. "I need to get a bag together." Ten minutes later, I let myself into his flat and found him standing at the other end of the corridor starting a coughing fit. His chest was congested, and he excused himself to the bathroom where he hacked and coughed up for a while until he could clear his chest.

"Richard, can you manage? I'm parked a bit beyond the entrance gate. Do you need my arm?"

Richard looked dreadful. He was unshaven and ashen grey. I had never seen him like that before. He had the look of someone who might not have long to live but he refused my arm, and I went ahead to bring the car as close as possible. We passed the porter as he shuffled his way out and, with a look of alarm, he asked Richard how he was. "Not good," was the brief reply. I opened the car door and pushed the front seat as far back as possible while Richard put his walking stick in the back. I helped Richard draw his long legs into the seat well and drew the seat belt across his chest before allowing him to fasten himself in. He was still fumbling to fasten it when I started the engine and had to reach across to assist him.

I was very worried, and we drove in silence for a few minutes whilst he was struggling to breathe. I placed my hand on top of his as he rested it on his leg and drove as quickly as I could.

"Oh, Bob," he said between gasps," I've had enough - I don't want to live anymore - I'm nearly 90 - I've got nothing left." Richard had been battling since December when the pacemaker had punctured his pericardium and he'd had a wretched time for weeks as they tried to drain it of fluid. Now, he told me, he had been battling bronchial pneumonia for three weeks, with chest pains, and was coughing up blood.

I prayed aloud for him as we drove, for his present comfort and that Jesus would bring His peace in this time of trouble. "You haven't seen me like this, have you, Bob?" It was true. His skin looked thin and grey, disclosing blue veins on his temple, and I commented on his long stubble. "I can't shave. The electric shaver is no good when it gets this long. I can't pray. Do you think that will count against me?"

His voice was hoarse and weak. This was very much a Richard comment, and I knew, of course, it wouldn't 'count against him.' He simply looked too exhausted to put thoughts for prayer together and I told him not to worry about talking, but just to try and rest as we drove the twenty minutes to West Middlesex A & E.

"Richard, we haven't spoken for a few weeks, but I called you right at the moment you had had enough and were about to take yourself into hospital."

"Yes, I'm so grateful it was you, Bob."

"What I'm saying, Richard, is that I'm sure it was the Lord's prompting to call right then, exactly at the right moment. He knows what is happening, Richard. He is with you now, whether you feel that or not. He is going with us to the hospital, and He will be with you in hospital."

By the time we arrived, Richard seemed a little calmer. There were changes to the hospital entrances and parking because of Covid and we both got confused about how to get into A & E. I parked outside the main entrance, knowing that Richard couldn't make it far on his legs, and told him that I would get a wheelchair and wouldn't be long while he waited in the car.

Inside the foyer were floor footprints and a couple of Covid temperature scanners attended by a security man. It was a short wait to stand in front of the machine to be scanned, at which point my temperature showed 37 degrees and the screen flashed red and started to beep. It had been the hottest day of the year by far and I still had my hat, scarf, and coat on, being accustomed to the chilly spring days that had preceded.

I was asked to step aside and let a few others be scanned and pass through before trying again. Same thing. Red lights and more waiting. I was protesting that I was hot because of my clothes and started stripping as much as possible before being gestured to try another machine. Same again, and by this time I was muttering about needing to get a chair and to get someone outside into A & E urgently.

By the fourth temperature scan, it had dropped to 36.7 and I ran in to collect a wheelchair, but they were chained together requiring a coin to release, which I didn't have. I came back to the security guard to protest my problem and he gave me the loan of an unlock tool. By now, I had been inside the hospital for about 10 minutes and was getting really concerned about leaving Richard in the car on such a hot sunny morning, when I saw him totter in through the main entrance door.

I got him seated in the wheelchair with difficulty, trying to lift and position his enormous feet on the footrests, and we quickly set off, only to realise that we couldn't access A & E from inside that hospital entrance. When I enquired again at the security point, we were redirected 'back outside and to the right'.

Richard is a very big man and once we got up momentum with the chair it was hard to control. We set off as directed, down quite a steep ramp, which turned out to lead to nowhere but a locked door. It was just a piece of dead-end garden, with a ramped path, a quiet place for visitors to sit outside. Pushing him back up to the top of the ramp took a lot of effort and I was breaking into a sweat having donned my outdoor clothes again.

An adjoining ramp seemed to lead to A & E, but it had an adverse camber to its outer perimeter, and, at one point, I thought I was going to pitch Richard over the railings as we raced down out of control. Then, I couldn't get him over the threshold of A&E where the entrance was substantially blocked by a Covid security sign, sufficiently spaced for pedestrians but not a wheelchair. Finally, we both appeared at the front desk with me having less breath than Richard.

Richard let me do the talking: 90-year-old man - pneumonia, coughing blood, and so on. We were asked to take a seat and I got Richard a bottle of water from the machine, he hadn't yet had any drink that morning, but once we had settled and he had a few mouthfuls, he seemed a little calmer.

"I'd better call Nicola, Richard. Do you want to speak to her?"
"No, you call her, please."

Richard looked worried and lost in his thoughts and so I called his daughter, Nicci, to say that I had brought him in. We agreed that there was no point in her racing from work to join us until Richard had been examined and I could call her back with any news.

Richard was triaged through reception to a nurse and after about half an hour, his name was called, and I wheeled him to an examination room where a doctor was waiting.

"Hello, Dr Richard. I understand you are a chest physician, is that right?"

Richard summoned some strength and, now in his medical element, seemed to draw on his past seniority in the conversation that followed, though his breathlessness and difficulty in speaking were very evident.

"Yeah, long, long, long ago. St George's, Tooting." "That's where I trained," the young doctor offered. "Good for you. I trained at Hyde Park Corner. You don't know that, do you?" "That used to be St. George's, didn't it? Yes, yes, I am aware." "I'm also an FRCP," said Richard, "so it makes it easier to talk about this." "Do you still have your FRCP?" "Oh yes. I'm retired, of course. I can't do the validation anymore." "My name's Ned."

The doctor spoke with an Irish accent, and without leading any further, waited for Richard, no doubt aware that he was about to examine someone who was very senior in his day. With laboured breaths, Richard then proceeded to take charge of the conversation that followed the initial pleasantries.

"Ned, I am nearly 90 years old. I've been through the mill for the last while. I have no more reserves left. There's something going on in my chest. I just don't know what it is." "Are you happy for a medical student to be with us today?" Ned asked. "Of course, yes," Richard confirmed, as a young lady waiting behind us in the doorway walked forward, introducing herself as Annabel.

It was the first time I had seen Richard in his medical world and, though so obviously unwell, it seemed natural for him to take charge, and for Ned and Annabel to defer respectfully to him.

"I'm a third-year medical student," said Annabel. "Where are you training?" "Imperial," she replied, and Ned concluded introductions. "This is Doctor Richard Rondel. He's an FRCP physician, used to be a chest physician, trained at George's."

Ned's short intervention was enough for Richard to jump back in again.

"All I need to know is, what the hell's going on?" Richard said, directly but without any sense of impatience. "I have gone beyond making any form of diagnosis. When I presented on the ninth of March - with upper right chest pain, worse on inspiration, my G.P. and I - thought it was a pulmonary embolism. I came in here on the tenth - for six hours - and you did everything. Apart from some raised LFT's* - you didn't find anything. You did a chest x-ray - and told me it was normal." Richard's energy was draining fast while talking and he was now drawing gasps between every few words.

"I've written on the form there," Richard pointed to his reception admission form, "that on the fifteenth - a few days afterwards - I had a phone call to say - that they had looked again - and that there were some worrying things - and could I come in for a CT scan - as soon as possible - by which time - I was laid out - with pulmonary pneumonia - and I couldn't come. So, this is the first time – I've been well enough - to come." Richard paused to regather strength.

"The symptoms are no better. I've still got the pain. I've still got the haemoptysis.* I've probably got more breathlessness now - than at the beginning."

Richard lifted his hands slightly and let them fall to slap the tops of his thighs gently. "That's me done." There was a moment before he added, "And I'm frightened ... I'm frightened."

"I've had a look at your notes," continued Ned. "Ok, I think they said that there were some plaques on the x-ray, but they didn't know

---

*LFT: Liver function tests. Haemoptysis: coughing up blood.

what the cause of them was. My impression is that we probably need to do a high-resolution scan. As you know, haemoptysis has a wide differential and we need to know what that is."

"Does your scan have any chance - of showing whether my pericardial effusion* - has dried up?" asked Richard. "It was said to have dried - on the twenty-fourth of December, but I don't know whether - it's still part of the picture - or not."

"The high-res scan will show whether there is effusion, but when I saw your echocardiogram, it said that there was no longer an effusion."

"No? Good." Richard clearly understood medical implications but having found no answers from his own knowledge it must have left him both wondering and worried.

"So, as you are aware, my impression is that your breathlessness, with haemoptysis, is less likely to be from an effusion and more likely to be pulmonary in aetiology but we can investigate this for you."

"I'm not trying to be clever," Richard responded, "but is there any evidence of ST* depression on my ECGs?" "From memory, when I looked at your notes, you did have some ST changes. However, I will get one today and compare that. Do you have any chest pain now?"

"Only here." Richard pointed to his right upper chest.

"OK, I think we have an ECG from when you came last time with that pain, so we can compare that with today and see if there are any changes. We'll do a workup for you, OK? We'll take it from the beginning, and, with what we know about your history, we'll try to give you some answers." "I am *so* grateful to be here," Richard said. I

---

*Effusion: fluid filling the pericardial membrane.
*ST: Sinus Tachycardia (The natural pacemaker rhythm of the heart)

never saw him cry or release any emotion, but he was now clearly physically and emotionally spent. "Richard, I'll be honest with you," Ned said, "Haemoptysis is concerning, you know that." Richard steeled himself for a final question using medical shorthand for cancer.

"Is there any possibility of CA?" "Yes, there is a possibility. But there are also multiple other things that could be the cause of this. We will start with an ECG, continue with a chest x-ray, we'll do some blood work to check to see if you're anaemic; you seem a bit breathless to me. We'll do some observations and then we will discuss with the medics to see how we get the imaging done."

"Could I add in - I have a cervical kyphosis*, which makes it difficult for me to lie straight out - in the scanner. I've also got - a pinned fracture - of the left shoulder, and a healed spiral fracture - of the right humerus, and all that makes it claustrophobic - in the scanner - for a big chap like me."

"Our scanner is open-ended," Ned reassured. "Oh, good." "The scanning room is big, and the scanner is open." "I understand - I just thought I'd mention it." "Tablet wise, do you take a whole host of tablets? No, nothing?" Richard had shaken his head.

"Well, I would prefer to be without it, but I'm not going to - dig my heels in." "And the pacemaker was fitted how long ago?" "On the fourth of December. And as they fitted it, the atrial lead penetrated the pericardial membrane. And then I got a huge effusion - with tamponade*- and then they had to go in again - and replace the atrial

---

*Cervical kyphosis: When the top of the spine curves in the opposite direction to usual.
*Tamponade: A serious compression of the heart due to excessive pericardial fluid.

lead - and drain the effusion, and for the whole of January, I was on prednisolone and cortisol... so, you know...."

Ned completed the sentence, "You've had a rough ride. Look, I'll do my best." "Yes, of course you will." "And I'll make sure you get some answers. I'll find a space for you to get comfortable with a bed and chair and we'll start that way." "Fine", said Richard with his last bit of strength. "Sorry to bang on a bit."

I pitched in at the pause. "I'm a friend. I have called Richard's daughter. She is alerted, and I said either I would call her, or someone...?"

"Is your daughter medical?" Ned asked Richard. "No, she's legal." "Ok, I will call her." "Thank you."

I said my goodbyes to Richard, and, in parting, mentioned to Ned that we were writing a book together. "It's 90% finished. We have had a journey together."

"Is it creative writing or medical writing?" Ned asked. "A bit of everything," Richard said and began to speak of the Community Centre where we first met.

I mentioned that Richard used to bring us fresh trout for our homeless visitors, but then he and I went fishing and I asked if he wouldn't mind going on a kind of pilgrimage with me, whereby we would explore each other's lives and faith whilst allowing others to eavesdrop.

"It sounds wonderful, it sounds great. I would love to read it," Ned and Annabel said together. "Perhaps you will," I said, as I left the room. "Please make sure you look after him."

Richard's Mary called me the following Saturday having got my number from his daughter Nicci. She had tried before but couldn't get through. It was the first time we had spoken properly, and we chatted for half an hour or so. Richard was still in hospital, depressed because he just wanted to get back home, though slightly better now that they had moved him to a single room where he could see some trees. There was still no prognosis, though quite a large liver mass was definite, and some nodules and some cancer on the lung, and several pulmonary embolisms.

Mary called again a few days later because she had promised to update me after saying that there was some possibility Richard might be released home, but his oxygen levels had been low, and he was on morphine. She sounded very tired and told me that there was a cancer mass on his liver which was quite large, extending the liver membrane and giving him pain. Richard had to be persuaded that staying in hospital was best for now. 'He's so stubborn!' she had said. 'All he wants to do is get home,' and we amused ourselves at imagining the kind of conversations he might be having, pulling his retired rank with the doctors and nurses.

Besides, she continued to say that there was no food at home, carers had to be organised and it was likely that he would require oxygen and some sort of help day and night. But there was still no prognosis, and Mary voiced her frustration at the hospital that she could get no information from anyone.

She called again quite late on Sunday evening and wanted to let me know that Richard was coming home on Monday. "But he looks awful," she said. "They haven't looked after him, and I'm so cross about it. He's not been shaved, and he's very worried and upset about everything. Anyway, I just wanted to let you know, Bob. Would you perhaps wait until the Tuesday before you call round? That way we can get the flat sorted and, you know, make him look a bit more himself." Her voice was shaky, and she seemed exhausted.

I called Richard's house phone on Tuesday afternoon and Mary picked up. She spoke to Richard to say who it was, and I heard his voice in the background. He sounded wretched and weak.

"Oh, I should have called you, Bob," said Mary. "There was a bit of a hiccup and Richard has only just come home today. We are in the midst of trying to sort things out. Perhaps tomorrow?" I could hear on the phone that she gained some assent from Richard for the following day and so I said goodbye, and that I would call again. I had not known what to expect but I could hear from the sound of Richard's voice in the background that, most likely, my old friend as I had known him had now gone, and that same Richard would not be coming back.

I tried again on Wednesday while walking the river towpath and Nicola picked up. "Bob," she said, "it is some good news and some bad. The good is that he has a really good care package that we have managed and the main lady in charge seems very competent. The bad news is that she feels he may pass as soon as early next week. Can you come tomorrow afternoon?" We arranged that I would call to see if he was awake and come round at short notice if he was.

I spent half an hour or so walking the Thames River path by Richmond Bridge where Richard and I had walked together many times and chatted and sat at the cafés. The riverfront was packed on a sunny day as people were beginning to come out of Covid lockdown. Children were feeding the ducks and a heron stood on the embankment edge. The man at the fruit juice stall, the boat repairmen next to their open workshop arches, and a busking musician, all signified that life was going on. My emotions began to rise as I thought about our friendship, that I wouldn't walk that path with Richard again and that the pages of our last chapter together were turning to their end. I was anxious to see him. I was anxious to know what might happen,

Between then and the following afternoon, I spent much of the waking time with Richard on my mind and with frequent prayer, and some concern about how I would find him and what I could say. I wondered whether he would be able to talk, and a whole range of jumbled and worried thoughts came to mind about what might be our last visit together, if I could get to see him in time.

Chapter 34.

Un Fuerte Abrazo

By the time I was parking up and due to knock at 2.30 on Thursday afternoon, I was feeling nervous. I hadn't been nervous about seeing Richard since that lunch nearly six years previous when I had asked him to embark on this 'project' as he called it.

The key was still in his door as usual. I rang the bell rather than knocked and to my surprise, I thought I heard Richard shout as best he could to let myself in, which I did.

He was in the living room at the end of the corridor. The door was open, and I could soon see that the room had been rearranged to accommodate a hospital bed right in the middle, where his mahogany coffee table had been. Richard was in grey and white checked pyjamas, propped with some pillows behind him, and with his back to the window. A frame over his legs elevated a red tartan blanket that covered his lower half and he had air tubes in his nostrils, and a little dried blood on his lower lip, but otherwise, he was shaved, his hair was brushed, and he looked better than the day I had taken him to A & E.

There was a considerable amount of noise and activity. The oxygen machine by his bed was breathing and whirring between bleeps and two men were coming and going between the front door and the kitchen where they were finishing the fitting of a countertop dishwasher.

Mary was still hovering, having made the arrangements for fitting the dishwasher and she and Nicci promised to leave us in private. I greeted them both with a brief re-acquaintance chat after not seeing them since his 85th birthday.

"Bob," Richard said softly, and continued between laboured breaths. "You're a little bit early. Do you have papier mâché urine bottles at the Vineyard?"

I was a bit surprised by his first greeting but soon realised that he was stalling until we had privacy. Nicci overheard and said that she had done some research and had ordered some. After a few minutes, the workmen left, Mary and Nicci went out to shop, and we were left alone.

I brought a chair from his nearby dining table and placed it next to the bed and reached for his hand. Richard was weak and breathless and had to measure his words with short sentences and pauses and with some effort. "I would normally offer you a cup of tea," he said. "I'm attached to tubes - and couldn't get up anyway. You can see the oxygen cylinder."

"Richard, I'll make one later. I just want to see you. It must be about two and a half weeks since that trip to A & E." "Yes," he said. "I was lucky. I don't want to - go into it too much. I was lucky - to get out - of hospital. It was a nightmare. We had to fight - every inch - of the way. There were six bays. Two other men - like me - constantly -

asking- the staff- to let them die. And the system - is totally geared - against it. I can understand - the legal- implications. Be careful - what you wish for. Two - of those men - were worse - than I was - and hardly- had breath to speak. And no one - to speak for them. Without Mary - and Nicci - I would still be there. There are instructions- plastered on the walls - all over Richmond. I must never leave this room. I'm here to die." Richard squeezed my hand a little before saying, "And looking forward to it."

Richard looked at me and smiled. "Nicci could tell you. This flat has been- in constructive - glorious turmoil - to get everything right, Bob. First thing. I want to send - a long email."

Richard's hands trembled as he picked up the iPad on his lap. "This is the address." He fumbled with his device for almost a minute trying to open up an email tab. "I can't think so fast," he said, as he struggled with it for a while longer and then gave up and handed the iPad to me. "I'm going to send a message. The message is to: A.N.A., M.A.R.I. He spelt the letters out individually and it was then I realised that he wanted me to write to his dictation.

"What's the subject?" I asked. "'Blanca. Pamplona. Long- years- of friendship.' I'll outline - and you'll have to do - the clever stuff," he said, and then we spent the best part of half an hour composing no more than a few paragraphs for a letter to Ana Mari, the sister of his second wife, Blanca, who had died suddenly with a brain tumour. Richard's hands were now frail, but he was still sharp in mind, and he spent a considerable time minutely scrutinising every comma, checking the grammar, and spelling, and rephrasing every line of this private letter. 'Dear Ana Mari,' he started, and then placed me as the writer in the first person before he continued, 'I have been Richard's closest friend - for many years and know more about Richard's life than anybody else. He has asked me to say goodbye to you - because he is dying....' Even though breathless, Richard spoke faster than I could type on the unfamiliar keypad, even between his very laboured breaths. When the letter was finished, he asked, "Are we done? I don't know how to finish it. You can't just send best wishes."

I suggested that there should be a closing sentence. He had said he was dying and perhaps there should be something to reassure. "Richard, you just told me that you were looking forward to dying. Would you perhaps like to close by saying that you are at peace?" "Yes," he said. "Yes. That would end it. The Spanish are not sentimental - especially the northern Spanish. They're Navarrese. I don't want anything mushy." And after my suggestion he added a final phrase in Spanish: 'Un fuerte abrazo.'

"How do you spell that?" I asked. "I thought you spoke Spanish?" "Not yet, Richard. I would like to for my grandson, but not yet." "A big hug," he said. "It means - a big hug." He spelled it out and I typed. "And I suppose you should add - my name at the end: 'Richard.'"

I read it all through aloud one more time, and then Richard took the tablet and also read it through himself one last time, paying meticulous attention to every word. It had only been a few sentences, but it all took well over half an hour as Richard had read and reread the letter slowly. "Make sure she replies to you, Bob, not to me." I added that request, and then we pressed send.

"Now, Bob - I had all these notions - of being buried at sea - but I had a long talk with Nicola - and Mary. Nicola is an amazing woman - and I have said to Mary - I beseech you to arrange for me - the cheapest possible funeral. You need the money - more than the undertakers. Therefore, a cremation. Some time ago - Nicci and I called in - and visited my old church, All Saints at Springfield. I have asked Nicci, Mary and Mark, that my ashes - be scattered over that church ground, - it's our village church. I will be there with all the people - that I knew and grew up with - and that's the right place for me. That community, that village - and church - made me. I'll try to show you - a couple of things, Bob."

Richard reached for his iPad again and opened up some photos. "That's our lych-gate. That is the seat I sat in - as head choirboy. That is the churchyard, beautifully preserved. They haven't been asked yet. I hope that they will allow it - the sprinkling. People can come. I don't want - one of those services - where people say - nice things about you. I want to be remembered - as coming out of that earth. My home was 400 yards - down the road.

"The churchyard is beautiful - isn't it? It's where I want - people to wander round - and talk about me - if they want to. And you'll be there."

"I will be, Richard."

"Now, Bob, I want to say - what you already know. I walked out on Mary - to be with Blanca - in 1990 I think it was - and left them - and I didn't do it well." Richard choked for a moment before recovering. His ability to swallow and his breathing were laboured. "Blanca died - in October 2006 - and over a long period of time - we have rebuilt our family, not thanks to me - but thanks to the love - and generosity of spirit - that forgave me - allowed me to re-join - the family. For the last 10 years or so, - to my amazement - we have been a family again. I have done everything I can - to repay them - for something that cannot be repaid - it overawes me. And I have left every penny - for Mary. "They have to know - how much - I have been overwhelmed - by their love. You know me, Bob. I never expected - their generosity of spirit. It's stronger than mine."

Richard rested for a few moments and then said, "Are we done?" "I'm going to make a cup of tea and give you a few minutes to rest," I said, and went to the kitchen and made myself a cup to let Richard recover from his exertion, and soon returned to his bedside. "I wanted to ask you, Richard, if there is anything else I can do for you. We do know and love each other." "Yes, we do - you are one of my greatest gifts - unexpected."

"And likewise," I said. "I feel quite emotional at the thought that we may not see each other much longer." "Surely - you're used to seeing - dying people - aren't you?" "It's not that, Richard. Even Jesus wept at the death of his friend Lazarus, knowing of course that he would raise him from life. No, it's death itself and the separation of the departed that causes the grief, even though we know we shall meet again. I want to know, Richard, that you are at peace and confident about your future."

"Yes, I'm looking forward to dying. You know my credo - from the book. I will tell you - what I asked for - in the hospital. I wanted one of those wooden crosses - with a little metal Jesus on it. I don't know how to put it, Bob. You must know - the depth of my religious being - better than anybody. And my dear chap. What a blessing it is - to have a conversation like this. In the old days - the parish priest - would have gone round. He would have known - a little about you. But this is unique. I'm compos mentis. I never expected - to be assailed - by sudden liver cancer, chest cancer, pulmonary embolism, all at once. I am a bag full of mess. And the sooner it is over, the better. It is a burden."

Richard paused from the effort of speaking. "It is a burden. I just hope it comes sooner - rather than later."

I hugged my dear friend gently and held his hand. His body's struggle to live and his own wishes to die were now all-consuming during his wakeful moments, but I was now settled in my own mind that he was looking to Jesus and would soon be with Him.

"The medical people - want to sustain you. That's the last thing I want."

"What I want for you, Richard, is that you would have a peaceful departure, with great expectation. The expectation that I have for you, Richard, and the one that even the thief on the cross was given by Jesus, is those words He spoke then: 'Truly, truly, today you will be with Me .... in Paradise." Richard completed the ending of that sentence as we spoke it together.

"Absent from the body, Richard, but present with the Lord. My prayer is that you would look towards that." "Of course, of course," Richard said. "I have many long hours - through the day - and night, to think about - nothing else."

"And there will be a great welcome for you, Richard. I know His love for you from the love in my own heart for you. I am so thankful that we have been friends."

"Yes. Yes." Richards' voice was barely audible now, his energy spent for that day, and his eyes closed for a few seconds. "It isn't over yet," he whispered, opening his eyes again, still with a hint of wry humour, and he was just starting a sentence about his mother dying of pneumonia at the age of 96 when we were interrupted by a knock at the door. It was the visiting carers who then came in.

"I don't have my daughter here - to interpret the situation," he said to them. "But for the moment - I'm comfortable."

Soon, Mary also arrived, but I asked for just a few more moments with Richard. They all retreated, and he continued where he left off.

"My mother was living - at my sister's home at Woking - but was sent to Battle Hospital - for the five days that it took her - to succumb, and on any - of those five days - there were members of the family - around. I spoke with her, I think, after three days there. It was about the last time - that was possible. It's that kind of thing - that I had envisioned. That people - in the old traditional sense - might gather round me. But it's hard to time. There's a paper on that table, Bob, that says - do not resuscitate. Everyone who matters - knows that I must never - leave this room. No matter what… now, where did we get to?"

"I wanted to pray with you, Richard." "Yes. Do, do." I began to thank God for Richard, but we were soon interrupted again by Mary who said the carers had thought they should come in anyway and it was now my time to retreat until they were done with checking his oxygen and his legs, which, when I came back a few minutes later, I overheard had dried out well from their fluid.

"This is my life at home," said Richard. "Constant traffic," and we attempted to resume.

"I started to pray for you, Richard."

"Yes, you did, and I'm very receptive."

I started again, thanking God for our friendship and our love for each other and I prayed that the Lord's presence would be very close, and for his family. Richard affirmed every phrase with, "Yes, yes," and when I had finished, he said that he hoped he would see me again soon, but neither of us could be certain of that.

I left, affirming my love for him and that he was much loved by his family, and the Lord, and I kissed his forehead. "This is a tremendous load off my mind," he said as I was parting. "As soon as you hear back - from Ana Mari - let me know."

I met Mary at the door as I left on that morning. She was 83 years old but looked younger, even in her obvious tiredness from the previous weeks. We chatted over this and that and how appalling she felt his hospital treatment had been. I told her that Richard was so enormously appreciative of her care and mentioned his constant incredulity that the family had taken him back after how badly he had treated them. We spoke of his wishes to be scattered at Springfield Church and of how my father had wanted his ashes to be scattered over his favourite yellow rose bush in the front garden, but it was a windy day and so he ended up on the neighbours' car. We had laughed, and Mary said, "And never wear turn-ups when ashes are scattered!"

We nattered for a while and then I started to tell her that pretty much 90% of the book that I was writing had been finished. She looked quizzical and so I asked if she knew about the book. "No," she said. "Oh, you don't. Richard never said?" "No, he's funny. What's the book about?" I told Mary about how we met over a couple of donated trout and explained the format of the nature of its exploration of each other's lives. "Oh, he did mention something, but not much really. I'd like to see it if it's published," she said, and I promised that of course she would see it, even before that.

It was a couple of days before I could visit again. Richard was now expected to live a few more days than first thought, though there was a chance that he could pass away at any time. When we were alone, Richard directed me to find a black attaché case which was in a cupboard in his bedroom. I found it and brought it to him. It seemed locked but when the clasp was pressed sufficiently firmly, it opened to reveal several folders and files.

I brought the case back and he asked, "Do you have access to an incinerator?" "We have one of the garden ones, I think, at the church."

He rooted around in the case. "These are some negatives - of no consequence. Burn." And he handed them to me. "This is a photo of me with my Alvis." It was a wonderful-looking car, a mid-1930s version of the Alvis Speed 20 Vanden Plas Drophead Coupé, with a canvas top, running board, and a spare tyre mounted to the nearside of the bonnet. Richard had posed beside it, very suave, dressed in a suit and tie and with a handkerchief in his breast pocket.

There was another photo of his mother, and another posed on Westminster Bridge where he had his winter coat and leather gloves on, and the Houses of Parliament were in the background. There were one or two other black and white photos, one with a school girlfriend, and one reclined on the grass in a garden somewhere, where he looked as though he was about sixteen.

He found a file which he directed me to pass to Anna Baghioni who had been a librarian and historian in Jersey. There was some kind of project which she was doing on the Rondels. "She ought to see this," he said. "Tell her she can come and get it any time." Then

Richard asked me to get a larger case from the same cupboard, a black flight bag.

"It's heavy, Richard. Is it ok for you if I open it up on your lap?" I opened the bag up for him, along with its various zip pockets and Richard began to look through old brown and yellow Kodak wallets that contained prints in one pocket and the negatives in another.

He sorted through them slowly, with long reminiscing smiles as he gazed at each one, before passing them to me and saying, 'destroy.' There were also some items for his son Mark, some photos for Julie, his sister, and some for the family, but mostly, minute by minute, for a long time, he looked at the mementos of his Spanish liaison with Blanca and her family, before handing each to me saying, 'destroy.'

There were a few items to send to Ana Mari, photos of her sister Blanca which Richard had taken in Paris and Spain. Occasionally, Richard said, 'she would love that one', or 'those are for Ana Mari.' Occasionally he paused with long sighs over each of several black and white photos from years ago. Sometimes, under his breath, he whispered, "Dear Blanqui, -dear Blanqui."

He showed me one photo. "This was the flat we converted in Spain. And this was Blanqui shortly before she died. She had a cerebral tumour."

Eventually, Richard had been through everything. "So, everything is done?" "Yes," I said, and I went through every compartment of the case taking his instructions as he opened each wallet and file. There were also his expired passports in the other attaché case. "Ah yes, my life history," Richard mused, but apart from that, it looked as though we had been through everything.

By the time he had finished, I had separated his various instructions into all the pockets of the case. It was full again and I needed it to carry everything away.

He seemed relieved that this great effort had concluded. "So much of what needed to be done is done... so that it didn't hurt anybody. I have days of wondering - about how I was deceitful, but the answer to that is - that my family took me back. They forgave me. God is good."

"Yes," I said, "God is good. He is all about reconciliation. He longs for reconciliation." "Yes, yes," Richard agreed. "I don't know whether - I want you - to pray with me - or over me." "Let's do both," I suggested.

Richard was almost out of breath in these last words that day, and very emotional. Clearly, he had voiced the same grace that God has for each of His prodigals as he related his extreme gratitude for the reconciliation offered by his family. He seemed incredulous that they had received him back. Trespasses had been forgiven, in spite of the wrongdoing that he so intensely recognised.

I asked if Richard wanted to talk to the Lord about this. "I don't really have any regrets," he said. "I have the knowledge of things..." There was a long pause. "I can't find the words," he said. This visit had so tired him.

I began to pray for him. "Lord, we pray together ...," and I thanked Jesus that Richard was forgiven and prayed for his increasing peace as he approached this life's end. I gave thanks for his life and the life that the Lord had planted within him, and Richard interjected, "That he has so generously given me." "There will be no more tears and no more pain," I continued. "Richard awaits the beauty of the resurrection, Lord. He looks forward to coming and being with You."

"I do - I do," he managed to rasp.

"And you, Lord, look forward to greeting him. It will be face to face, no more through the glass darkly. I know that He will be with you and that He and I will also be together for a new and better chapter to come." "Yes, yes!" Richard's voice was very faint.

"I want to thank you for the friendship that we have had over these five or six years," I continued, and I held Richard's hand as we prayed. As I touched his arm, I could feel through his pyjamas the lump where his arm had healed. "I thank you, Jesus, that you healed Richard's arm."

"Yes! Yes. I remember!" Richard's voice suddenly came out strong as he joined with this particular thanksgiving. With my words, we were both praying together. I thanked the Lord for the few times we had managed to fish together, and to sit down for that lunch when I asked him if we could begin this journey and how he had sat back to wipe his mouth with his napkin and said, "When do we begin?"

"Thank you, Lord, that we did begin, and that there will not be an ending. I bless Richard and I commend him to you, Jesus. Amen."

"Amen," said Richard. "Give my love to Enid." "Yes, I will."

"Now rest, Richard. This has been so tiring for you. I hope to see you in a day or two."

I doubted I would see him again, kissed his forehead in leaving, as I had done every time since seeing him on his return from hospital, and departed carrying the case.

Chapter 35.

The Lord Has Spoken

Nicci was waiting outside and felt that I should explain the suitcase I was carrying. I gave her various bundles that were designated for Mark and other family members, but the main compartment was filled with what Richard had asked me to destroy: his affairs and mementos from Blanca and the Spanish side of his life. I opened the case so that she could glance at it and explained that Richard had given it all to me to burn, but only because he presumed that there might be hurt, and he didn't want that.

Nicci said she was curious, and also that there was nothing unknown or unforgiven between her and her father. We could both see the dilemma that I hadn't expected to be in: to take note of the wishes of my dying friend, or on the other hand, what was clearly the hope of his daughter that she might get to look at the mementos of her father. If I was in her position, I would be the same. Here was a relatively new acquaintance carting off a case of her father's most personal mementos. I had no idea what the case contained, what was written in the large bundle of letters from Blanca, or the piles of photos, and we talked a while around this dilemma. What to do?

I said that I wouldn't destroy it all straight away but would take a look and we could talk again about whether she could have all or some of it. I needed to ponder and pray on whether to take account of the wishes of the living, or the departed, especially since it seemed likely, in Nicci's case at least, that these were mementos that might be precious to her and not wounding, as her father supposed.

When I came again two days later, Richard was weaker still and asleep. I chatted briefly with Nicci to explain possible funeral arrangements and offered to help in any way the family wanted.

I called by again in the afternoon, but he was still asleep. Richard was now gaunt. He had not had food for days and his face was shrinking to his skull making his teeth more prominent. His mouth was always open as he took shallow breaths. No doubt his great frame that had often enveloped me with a hug was also shrinking beneath the sheets.

Richard's son, Mark, was in the room as I sat down by his bed and held his hand while he slept but Richard promptly opened his eyes.

"Hello, dear friend."

"I've just come to say a quick hello, Richard. I came this morning, but you were snoozing." "Richard struggled to talk. It was now just one word at a time between gasps and sometimes a brief retch. "Are there - any - loose - ends - still - untied?"

I asked Richard if the package arranged by Anna Baghiani had arrived from Jersey. It had. It was the Rondel family Bible, and Mark got up to retrieve it from a nearby table and passed it to me. It was a heavy and somewhat tatty Bible, about 4" in depth, and with some leaves a bit out of place. I took a glance and saw that it was printed in

Paris in 1825. "In French. Of course," said Richard, "It's a weighty tome, a pulpit Bible, not a pocket one."

Richard turned to Mark who was sat on the sofa. "Bob has - French ancestry." Mark and I chatted a while about my great uncle Albert and his celebrated flights in South Africa and France. It was probably all a bit much for Richard and when Mark and I had finished chatting he said, "I have - moments now - when I feel - ghastly." Ever the doctor, Richard offered a diagnosis. "I think - it's the liver - failing."

"I should go, Richard, you are so tired." "No. Stay." "For a while then. I am just going to be dropping in from time to time."

I turned to Mark. "If your dad is awake, I will let him know I'm here and hold his hand, as I am now. Is there anything more you want from me now, Richard?"

"Just to pray. If Mark doesn't mind."

"It doesn't matter whether he minds or not," I said, in a tone that brought a chuckle from us both.

"Please ask the Lord - to take away my nausea," Richard asked. He was clearly very uncomfortable. I prayed, acknowledging that a much greater comfort would soon be coming, but also asking that Richard would find relief and peace as his body entered that stage of discomfort he was experiencing while conscious. His body was now shutting down quite rapidly. No doubt he had seen the same thing many times as a ward doctor.

The last time I saw Richard was three days later. His carers had sorted his nausea with medication, he continued with the morphine patches, and he was slowly slipping away. Various arrangements to visit earlier were postponed to allow family members to attend and they told me that he was sleeping for long periods.

On the 25th of April, as Enid and I were passing to take a walk nearby in Richmond Park, I thought I would just drop in for just a few moments on the off chance. I knocked gently, let myself in with the key as usual, and crept in to sit down beside him. Richard soon woke. "Oh, Bob! How nice - of you to come." Every word was a struggle through dryness, and he seemed much too weak to talk.

"I have - something - I wanted - to ask you. A connection. But - I have - forgotten. I can't remember. Have you - only - got - two seconds? Want - a cup - of coffee?"

Even in this extremity, Richard was trying to be hospitable, but it was clearly frustrating him that he couldn't remember the thing that must have occurred to him. "I might get - Nicola - to text you- if - it crops up."

"You're sleeping quite a lot now, Richard," I said. "Yes, I am," he said. "Sliiiding away. Not long now." He managed a grin with his drawing out the 'sliiide...' There was an expectation of relief with the finishing line coming into sight.

As we continued, Richard was surprised to hear it was Sunday, and that Mark was also there.

"Joy's bouquet - lasted - and lasted," he said. "Is that what you wanted to remember, Richard?" "Yes!" he said. "Please tell her."

Richard's hair had grown uncut for several weeks but was brushed neatly and lying either side of his head on the pillow. "I haven't seen your hair so long, Richard. You look like a bit of a rock star, a diva." I told him what I had preached on that morning, from the Sermon on the Mount in Matthew chapter six, all about the heart.

There was a pause and Richard asked me to bestow my blessing on him. "Yes, of course, Richard. May I read something to you first?" "Yes, please do," he replied, "whatever - you would like."

I searched on my phone Bible app to find 1 Corinthians chapter 15 about the resurrection of the dead and read from verse 35. Richard listened attentively to all that was being recounted concerning his own death and resurrection, his perishable nature to be clothed with the imperishable, his mortality with immortality, the great victory won through our Lord Jesus Christ. He had a great smile on his face as I was finishing. "Oh, Bob," he whispered, and those were to be the last words I heard from him.

Further visits were put off because he was nearly always asleep. I kept hoping for one last time but a week later, as I was half asleep on the Bank Holiday morning, I was praying for Richard and sensed a very joyous presence of the Lord. It was more than that, and whether I was awake or half asleep I could not tell, but I sensed a joyous and peaceful presence of the Lord, together with Richard being present. It was as though he, I and the Lord were together.

For several days I had expected a call from one of the family to say that Richard had died, and all the more so in that last week. I think it had been a surprise to everyone that he had lasted so long, and so I was fully expecting a call that May Bank Holiday Monday, but none came. Then, on Tuesday, May 4th, I had a morning text from Nicci: 'Dear Bob, just to let you know that my dad died yesterday evening. He was unconscious and just slipped away.......'

It was expected, of course, but the note still brought a great wave of sadness, and also gratitude that we had been able to draw so close almost to the very end. There would be funeral arrangements, people to write to that he had put me in touch with, medical colleagues, people in Spain and some local contacts, but I felt the profound sense of loss that everyone does when someone close departs. My reading that morning had been from Isaiah 25.8.

'...*He will swallow up death forever. The Sovereign Lord will wipe away the tears from all faces; He will remove His people's disgrace from all the earth.*

The Lord has spoken.'

***

Epilogue

Marlino!

Two, perhaps three miles out to sea, beyond the reef and Zapatillas,
Bocas' dual footprint, sand-edged jewels with jungle centre trees,
Francesco's outboard boat heads out to Caribbean's deeper blue.
Here sun burns softer gringo skin, tho' canopy saves that paining hue
from deceiving rays, bounced bright-reflected by glass-gentle waves.

Francesco's legs look saddle bent, as though a horse-led life was spent
beneath his gaucho hat, but though he had not spoken,
others spoke of bones not set, that hands and feet were broken.
Francesco lived not on a ranch but on a floating island,
mangrove's root and branch, no higher than his hut front door.
His wife, and children out of school, wait daily setting sun's return
of father-fisher, pescador.

Indian-brown and weather-beaten, today he boats pale gringo,
whose wallet dollar pays a better sum, whose wife and daughter take the sun,
reclined with son on one of Caios Zapatilla's footprint sand-lined jewels.
They await their fishing father, and anticipate his late return
with another disappointing tale.

El Nina's year, with weather clearer, girl-child brings the fish much nearer.
With Zapatillas out of sight soon deeper water's darker light
sees first the baitfish shoaling past, and then the Spanish Mackerel.
Wahoo at last begin to show, dark shadow's silent glide below
Francesco's twelve-foot boat.

And there is a quickening of hope, a hope of fishermen's vainglory,
a hoped-for fully laden boat, a hope of bolder stories told
as children hear their fishing fathers' words unfold,
and thankful wives will find, and finely hone,
their sharpest fillet knives.

Captain Francesco follows caravanning lines of fish,
and gringo casts his fishing line and makes his silent wish.
But soon the baitfish, drop-netted from the mangrove margins,
and sloshing in their water hold, are lost to Wahoo's razor teeth
which cut the line and take the lot 'cause they forgot the wiry trace.

At last, a single fish on board, and that because the line is caught
and wrapped around its tail. But hooks and bait have almost gone,
and soon they both must head for home.

Though on the way, a final try. A shark hook find
amid assorted debris stowed, and with a fillet cut from fish's tail,
the rig is starboard pitched and trolled some fifty yards behind.

Tired gringo sits to find the shade and eyes begin to glaze
in hottest part of midday's sun, and shimmered haze
with outboard's throttled churning hum
the only sound, as fishing day is done.

Eyes droop but still they look, and scan just one last time,
and find a dorsal fin to trail where hook and bait must be,
with black and waving tip of tacking tail close following behind.
At once alert. No sooner gringo points than rod is slammed
down to the gunwale. Reel screams, sparking nylon from reel's funnel.

Falling bruising to his knee and nearly pitching to the sea - the gunwale
tips to water's level, nearly losing man and rod as propeller tops
and breaches wavy trough, the engine screams its airy throttle.
Francesco's hand-hold grip is lost.

Then slack. Slack just for a moment, as flimsy boat returns upright,
but barely seconds pass before the line is tight and muscles drenched
and muscles clenched are taught, and breaching port, just front of prow,
fish shape begins his freedom leap.

Fishing for Dr Richard

Marlino!

Francesco shouts from back of boat as black-backed sail and tail and bill
all mighty leap, and iridescent body stripes hang high to crest his arc,
and bold black eye comes eye to eye with gringo as tormentor.

Then, leaping arc's momentum takes a downward path
to enter scarcely with a splash sleek fish's depthward pass,
and once again boat's jolting lurch tips gringo to his arse.

Now the reel begins to strip. Francesco, pescador, wheels to point the
prow and follow diving fins towards their darker sunless deep,
towards their deepest seabed floor.

Direction changes out to sea, all shadow gone from canopy,
and gringo bids Francesco's hat to shield the burning sun
as both are sat and balanced in the follow.

The steady stripping line begins to sing.
Elastic stretched to breaking strain with whine in gentle wind,
no inch of gain on diving fish and yard by yard the pull is hard
and muscles feel the pain.

Boat prow is tipped by downward pull and steady cuts slight waving
blue as time stands still, close heading for the hour before a word is said.
'How big?' The gringo's question comes, with no more power,
his legs are dead, his arms are numb. '400 pounds!' comes the reply.

And gringo thinks they both might die. But reel has peeled close to the
core, and soon the line will be no more, and fish will hold,
or fish will snap, but either way a story told,
composed far longer miles in heading back.

And then the moment comes. All line is out and rod still bends
to touch the gliding sea and descends a little further.
Francesco slides to balance port as boat tips close to water's edge
with gringo braced to what is caught, both arms wet in salty water
The line ascends its whining pitch.

Then snap. Then slack. Then gringo falling on his back.
Great fish was caught, and played,
And now there is a longer tack to Zapatilla's islands
while fish has found his freedom day within the deep blue ocean.

Wahoo's skin has dried, and skin and eye have lost their shimmered
iridescence. And beauty's essence of that fish has died beneath the
burning sun.

Yet, Marlino's sleek and black bold eye makes a story for the family,
a story for the son.
Paco, pescador Francisco, sits patting gringo's aching back.
He sits with him in silence, and silence says: well done!

***

Professor Richard Rondel 1931 – 2021   *Bob Kimmerling*
MBBS, Dip.Pharm.Med., Dip.Obst.
RCOG, FRCP, FFPM

Since 2003, Bob Kimmerling has been a minister and elder at the Vineyard Life Church in Richmond, Surrey, UK. He is a founder director of several local charities helping those in crisis and in poverty. Bob also writes poetry, loves fishing, and is hugely grateful for God's continuing work of grace.

Bob would love to hear from you if you want to connect:
- fishingfordr.richard@gmail.com
- Twitter: @Fishing4Richard

Lightning Source UK Ltd.
Milton Keynes UK
UKHW022010251121
394507UK00008B/143